REFORM, REVOLUTION, AND OPPORTUNISM

DEBATES IN THE SECOND INTERNATIONAL, 1900–1910

Edited by Mike Taber

Haymarket Books
Chicago, IL

Published in 2023 by
Haymarket Books
P.O. Box 180165
Chicago, IL 60618
773-583-7884
www.haymarketbooks.org
info@haymarketbooks.org

ISBN: 978-1-64259-981-7

Distributed to the trade in the US through Consortium Book Sales and Distribution (www.cbsd.com) and internationally through Ingram Publisher Services International (www.ingramcontent.com).

This book was published with the generous support of Lannan Foundation, Wallace Action Fund, and Marguerite Casey Foundation.

Special discounts are available for bulk purchases by organizations and institutions. Please email info@haymarketbooks.org for more information.

Cover artwork: Colorized photo of Rosa Luxemburg speaking at a public rally in Stuttgart, Germany, held in conjunction with the 1907 congress of the Second International. The original image is from the International Institute of Social History (Amsterdam), call number BG A40/996.
Cover design by Eric Kerl.

Library of Congress Cataloging-in-Publication data is available.

10 9 8 7 6 5 4 3 2 1

Praise for *Reform, Revolution, and Opportunism*

"Through this engaging volume, Taber has provided a tremendous resource to the socialist movement and historians of the Second International."

—**Eric Blanc,** author of *Revolutionary Social Democracy: Working-Class Politics Across the Russian Empire, 1892-1917*

"Debates in the European congresses of the Second International from 1900 to 1910 might seem a long way from the Bolshevik Revolution in 1917. Yet the Bolsheviks themselves self-identified very strongly as the Russian representatives of 'revolutionary Social Democracy' in contrast to international 'opportunism.' They insisted that the collapse of the Second International in 1914 was (in Lenin's words) 'the collapse of opportunism'—*not* the collapse of revolutionary Social Democracy. Mike Taber's invaluable presentation of the clash between the two wings of the Second International on vital issues such as war, colonialism, and women's suffrage is therefore essential reading for all who seek to understand the outlook of the Bolsheviks and their revolutionary tactics in 1917."

—**Lars T. Lih**, author of *Lenin Rediscovered*

"These excerpts from the debates at some of the most important congresses of the Second International allow us to see as never before how socialists of the time responded to such crucial issues as supporting anticolonial struggles and women's rights while opposing militarism and restrictions on immigration—the very issues being so heatedly debated today."

—**Peter Hudis,** general editor, *The Complete Works of Rosa Luxemburg*

"This book is a treasure chest for every socialist seeking to understand the history of their movement. Bringing together documents from 1900 to 1910, Mike Taber shows us how socialists more than a century ago analyzed and debated key questions of their time. He also shows us that these are urgent questions for *our* times: war and militarism; colonialism; immigration; gender rights; and strategies for working-class power. *Revolution, Reform, and Opportunism* is an invaluable contribution to the history of the socialist movement and Taber does a superb job of illuminating the context of these debates and showing us why they matter today."

—**David McNally,** author of *Blood and Money*

"Mike Taber offers clear and compelling translations of pivotal debates in the Second International around colonialism, immigration, women's suffrage, militarism, and political tactics during the first decade of the twentieth century. The debates reflect tensions between some socialists' racist, nationalist, and misogynistic prejudices and others' internationalism and desire for the liberation of both working men and working women. The selections in this book illuminate the roots of the 1914 split in the Second International and are relevant to struggles in our time."

—**Barbara C. Allen**, editor of *The Workers' Opposition in the Russian Communist Party: Documents, 1919-30*

"Many activists of today face challenges bedeviling socialists a hundred years ago: What should be the relationship between reform and revolution? To what extent should socialists adapt to existing power structures in the quest to ease the impact of multiple crises—and to what extent should they instead redouble their efforts to end the system generating such crises? Mike Taber draws together transcripts of rich and sharp debates from the mass-based Socialist International from 1900 to 1910—a clash of analyses and proposals offering insights to those of our own time who want to change the world."

—**Paul Le Blanc**, editorial board member, *The Complete Works of Rosa Luxemburg*

"In bringing together the key debates of the Second International in the first decade of the twentieth century, Mike Taber reveals the extraordinary nature of this movement. It is a fascinating and compelling read...Some of the challenges within the Second International are still with us today. This book gives us a chance to reappraise our history and its relevance for today."

—**Anne McShane,** historian of the Soviet Women's Movement

"Mike Taber provides yet another illuminating collection of documents, adroitly introduced and carefully compiled. *Reform, Revolution, and Opportunism* breathes contemporary life into the seemingly timeless clash of revolutionary and reformist sensibilities. Vexing matters such as war and militarism, colonialism and immigration, women's rights and strategic engagement with bourgeois states remain contentious today. Taber skillfully shows how a mass socialist movement once vigorously debated and disagreed about how to approach these matters."

—**Bryan D. Palmer**, author of *James P. Cannon and the Emergence of Trotskyism in the United States, 1928-1938*

"This book is a must-read. It provides a long overdue wake-up call for the Marxist left, which almost universally dismisses the experience of the Second International as inherently opportunist, with the failures, betrayals, and collapse of August 1914 supposedly written into this body's DNA. This book underscores just how flawed such an understanding is. The Second International was no monolithic or immutable entity sleepwalking into support for imperialist butchery but a hotbed of factional struggle waged by the forces of 'revolutionary social democracy'—Russian Bolshevism included—against the opportunist cancer that eventually killed it off. As Taber shows, the leading lights of the revolutionary Marxist tradition never renounced the best aspects of the International's political legacy but fought for its basic principles to be upheld in the face of the renegade, careerist, and nationalist 'socialists' who betrayed them."

—**Ben Lewis,** founder of *Marxism Translated*

"Over a century ago, socialists wrestled with many of the same questions and conflicts as we do today: how to understand and respond to intra-imperialist war, immigration from capitalism's periphery to core, colonialism and solidarity with and from the colonized world, women's rights, and women's roles in movements for liberation. By including primary source documents as well as speeches from socialists, including Rosa Luxemburg, Clara Zetkin, August Bebel, Karl Kautsky, Daniel De Leon and others, one feels the presence of live movements being made and remade in the crucible of fiery debate and struggle. Accompanied by Taber's lucid historical context, this selection of speeches and resolutions from the heyday of early twentieth-century socialism to its fracturing over World War I and reforming during the Bolshevik Revolution is a necessary read both for activists as well as scholars of these early battles against capitalism. Taber has offered twenty-first century socialists, if not a guide to the present, a helpful selection of examples of what earlier generations have exclaimed aloud, as in our world—still riven by war, imperialism, sexism, racism, class exploitation—the struggles and the movements for liberation must find their own answers and paths forward."

—**Benjamin Balthaser,** author of *Anti-Imperialist Modernism and Dedication*

"Mike Taber has made yet another major contribution—this time by resurrecting some of the earliest socialist debates on crucial issues that continue to challenge us today. This is a fascinating read and a valuable resource for contemporary activists."

—**Tom Twiss,** author of *Trotsky and the Problem of Soviet Bureaucracy*

"The 'experience of socialists a century ago can provide valuable lessons and examples' for socialists today because the emergence of the revolutionary trends within the Second International before 1914 anticipated those that arose in the aftermath of the October Revolution, as expressed in the formation of the Third International, writes Mike Taber. Whether Second International debates, in fact, contain invaluable, politically relevant lessons for communist activists today—or are of purely historical interest—is itself a matter of debate. Fortunately, Taber's documentary collection will help readers decide for themselves."

—**John Marot,** author of *The October Revolution in Prospect and Retrospect: Interventions in Russian and Soviet History*

Contents

3. The Debate on Immigration

4. The Debate on Women's Suffrage

5. The Debate on Militarism and War

Introduction

Why should readers today want to study debates in the Second (Socialist) International from over a century ago? Why should such debates be of interest to political activists in particular?

One reason for the relevance of this material involves the subjects under debate in the present book: war and militarism, women's rights, immigration, imperialism, and socialist tactics. All remain deeply contested issues and are scenes of ongoing political battle. Studying how an earlier generation of activists confronted these issues can therefore provide insight into socialist principles, tactics, and strategy.

Just as important, however, is the need to study the Second International itself. From 1889 to 1914 that organization, with all its strengths and weaknesses, was an example of a mass socialist movement, embracing the majority of the world's organized working class. Many thousands today aspire to just such a socialist movement, although their conceptions of it may vary widely.

Serious examination of the Second International, long overdue, is therefore of benefit to activists and scholars alike. My own efforts along these lines are registered in *Under the Socialist Banner: Resolutions of the Second International, 1889–1912*. Published in 2021 by Haymarket Books, that title collected together in a single volume—for the first time in English—all the resolutions adopted by the Second International's pre-1914 congresses.

The present book aims to extend that study by featuring excerpts from oral debates at four of these congresses. It is my hope that these two books, taken together, can make an important contribution to assessing the Second International and its legacy.

My aim, above all, is to show the Second International not just as a historical object worthy of study, but as a living *movement.*

A Revolutionary Working-Class Movement

The modern working-class movement emerged in Europe during the 1840s. Karl Marx and Frederick Engels provided this movement with a political and theoretical foundation, outlined in the Communist Manifesto, with its call of "Proletarians of all countries, unite!" The movement's goal was to be the revolutionary transformation of society, carried out by working people.

To advance toward that objective, Marx and Engels worked to promote international working-class organization. In 1847, they joined and became leaders of the Communist League, which had members in a number of European countries. Seventeen years later, in 1864, the two helped establish the International Workingmen's Association—better known subsequently as the First International—which set out to build a worldwide proletarian movement. Given the primitive state of early working-class organization, the First International had a short lifespan, existing only into the mid-1870s.

The late nineteenth century saw a major increase in the size of the working class in much of Europe and North America, along with the rapid growth of trade unions, socialist political parties, and other forms of proletarian organization. That growth made possible, in 1889, a resumption of the work of the First International on an even larger scale. Although lacking a formal name, the new movement was referred to as the Second International, acknowledging its continuity with the earlier world body. It was formed under the direct guidance of Engels, who, after Marx died in 1883 and until his own death in 1895, was the most widely recognized leader of the world socialist movement, known at the time as Social Democracy.

The Second International was born with an expressly revolutionary aim. A founding resolution declared that "the emancipation of labor and humanity cannot occur without the international action of the proletariat—organized in class-based parties—which seizes political power through the expropriation of the capitalist class and the social appropriation of the means of production."

The Socialist International of these years was, as registered in its adopted resolutions, an irreconcilable revolutionary opponent of the capitalist system. While it championed the fight for reforms in the interests of working people—the eight-hour day, state-sponsored insurance and pensions, public education, votes for women, the right to asylum, and many other reform measures—it rejected the idea that capitalism as a system could be reformed. It called for the working class to take political power and expropriate the capitalist owners of the major industries. It insisted that the working class itself was the agent of its own emancipation.

Strengths and Weaknesses

Over the course of the next quarter century, mass working-class parties affiliated to the Second International were built throughout Europe and North America. Many national trade union federations also adhered to it.

Perhaps the Second International's greatest achievement was to make progress in unifying the international working-class movement under the banner of Marxism. It also helped disseminate and popularize the movement's strategic aim: the revolutionary overturn of the capitalist ruling class and its replacement by the rule of the proletariat, as a first step toward the establishment of socialism.

The Second International showed the potential power of the organized working class, with tens of millions of members, sympathizers, and voters. Numerous socialist representatives and deputies sat in national parliaments and in regional and local legislative bodies.

Two dates on the calendar today owe their existence to the Second International: May Day, established at the International's founding congress in 1889 as a show of working-class power and solidarity around the world; and International Women's Day, created by the Socialist Women's Movement in 1910 as a worldwide day of action by working women in the fight for full social and political rights.

Along with these strengths and accomplishments, however, there were also important weaknesses that developed within the pre-1914 Second International.

For one thing, even though its resolutions called for the revolutionary replacement of capitalism, the Second International as a whole lacked a clear perspective on the role of revolutionary action in such a transformation. The relationship between reform and revolution became a constant point of friction and debate within its parties.

Another weakness involved the movement's geographic focus. Despite the fact that the Second International's reach extended to many countries, it was still predominantly a European and North American movement; in fact, it would never become a truly world organization. The only parties from outside Europe, North America, and Australia that were ever represented at Second International congresses during the 1889–1914 period were from Argentina, Japan, South Africa, and Turkish Armenia. While congress resolutions gave support to various anticolonial struggles, most sections of the movement still had an inadequate appreciation of them.

Similarly, the International's resolutions often lacked a sufficient assessment of the strategic allies the working class would need in its struggle—from toilers in the colonial world to working farmers and peasants, small shopkeepers, nationally oppressed peoples, and others.

Finally, the Second International came to be characterized by a gap between word and deed, as the day-to-day practice of most of its parties became increasingly dominated by currents with a reformist and nonrevolutionary outlook.

Trends in the Second International

The first open challenges to the Second International's expressed revolutionary perspective came to public attention in 1899: Eduard Bernstein's "revisionist" rejection of Marxism and Alexandre Millerand's becoming a minister in the capitalist government of France. These are both taken up in the first chapter of this book.

The debate over the perspective and the actions of Bernstein and Millerand was a heated one, involving almost all leaders of the world socialist movement. During the next several years, these two controversies spilled over to other issues as well. In these controversies a revolutionary and class-struggle perspective was counterposed to a class-collaborationist and opporunist one. A centrist middle current also eventually emerged, utilizing Marxist language while giving ground to the reformists in practice.

This division had social causes as well. The workings of imperialism tended to create privileges for a small layer within the working class of the more economically developed capitalist countries. This "labor aristocracy" became a base for opportunist leaders within Social Democratic parties and for a growing trade union bureaucracy, with a deeply class-collaborationist outlook on many questions.

Nevertheless, the Second International's unity remained unchallenged throughout this whole period. In the years prior to 1914, even those who would subsequently help create the Communist movement, such as V. I. Lenin and Rosa Luxemburg, never called for a split from the Second International. One reason for this unchallenged unity was that the Second International of the prewar period was not just an international organization of socialists; it was also seen as a sort of world parliament of the working-class movement. Maintaining the existence of this united body was considered by almost all socialists as virtually a matter of principle.

However, that unity came to a sudden end in 1914 with the onset of World War I.

Collapse and Split

In August 1914, the main parties of the Second International renounced past pledges to oppose capitalism's drive toward war and lined up behind their respective governments' efforts in World War I, voting for war expenditures and becoming ministers in capitalist governments. With the support of these parties' leaderships, millions of working people in uniform were sent to their deaths. Such actions were in direct violation of numerous resolutions adopted by international congresses. The Second International itself collapsed entirely, with its main parties supporting different sides in the conflict.

After 1914 the trends within the Second International crystallized into opposing international formations. The majority current gave outright support to the war effort of their countries' rulers, openly embracing a chauvinist perspective. While the centrist current did not go quite so far and criticized the most blatant aspects of the right-wing majority's conduct, it nevertheless tended to make excuses for these actions while aiming much of its fire at the left. Finally, the small but growing revolutionary left wing defended socialist internationalism.

The October 1917 revolution in Russia accelerated the international split. The entire working-class movement around the world eventually came down on one side or another: either support for the Bolshevik-led workers' and peasants' regime or opposition to revolutionary Russia and support for world capitalism's efforts to overthrow it.

The social democratic right wing, for its part, formally reconstituted the Second International in 1919. The new version of this body opposed

Bolshevik-led Russia as well as the postwar revolutionary upsurge that broke out in numerous countries of Europe and Asia. It became a loose coalition of parties aiming to reform and stabilize world capitalism. As for the centrist forces, in 1921 they created the International Working Union of Socialist Parties—popularly known as the Two-and-a-Half International. That organization had a brief existence, reuniting in 1923 with the Second International, which then relabeled itself the Labor and Socialist International (renamed the Socialist International after World War II).

The reconstituted Second International was far from the revolutionary movement formed in 1889. Rejecting the revolutionary goal adopted at the International's founding congress, it outlined instead a more modest and nonrevolutionary objective: "it is the historic mission of the Labour and Socialist International to defend the international proletariat against exploitation, repression, and violence."[1] For the next century, parties of the Second International shared in the administration of numerous capitalist states. They supported efforts to strengthen capitalism and opposed revolutionary movements around the world, backing numerous imperialist wars against oppressed peoples in Asia and Africa.

Meanwhile, the Third, Communist International (or Comintern) was founded in Moscow in March 1919. Presenting a balance sheet of the old International, V. I. Lenin wrote:

> The Second International is dead, overcome by opportunism. . . . The Second International did its share of useful preparatory work in preliminarily organizing the proletarian masses during the long, "peaceful" period of the most brutal capitalist slavery and most rapid capitalist progress in the last third of the nineteenth and the beginning of the twentieth centuries. To the Third International falls the task of organizing the proletarian forces for a revolutionary onslaught against the capitalist governments, for civil war against the bourgeoisie of all countries for the capture of political power, for the triumph of socialism![2]

Five Debates: Now and Then

This book features five debates on issues that remain scenes of struggle in contemporary society:

1. WAR AND MILITARISM

The twenty-first century has already been marked by armed conflicts of various types, from the US wars in Iraq and Afghanistan to conflicts in Syria, Ukraine, and elsewhere. In these wars working people and socialists have had to confront key questions: What is the cause of modern war? What position should working people take in each one? How can war be prevented? How should wars be fought once they begin?

The Second International debated these same issues at its congresses of 1907 and 1910. A range of positions were expressed—from those who saw little value in fighting the capitalist war drive, to some who called for answering war declarations with general strikes and insurrections. Questions such as demands for disarmament and international arbitration of disputes also came up, as well as the supposed distinction between "offensive" and "defensive" wars and the issue of "national defense."

2. WOMEN'S RIGHTS

At the present time, the right to abortion is at the center of the international fight for women's rights. In Argentina, Colombia, and Mexico, mass struggles have made advances in winning the right to abortion. Meanwhile, in the United States and Poland, steps have been taken to ban the procedure, leading to resistance and major battles beginning to unfold. Fights around other issues of women's rights have also occurred, such as equal pay, childcare, sexual violence and harassment, and society's gender norms. Such struggles have posed important questions for socialists: What is the cause of women's oppression? What role does it play in capitalist society? How can women's rights be won? In what ways is this fight interconnected with the working-class struggle?

In 1907, when the Second International congress took up the issue, the central question was for women's right to vote. The exchange at the congress around women's suffrage pitted uncompromising champions of this right against those who supported it but nevertheless viewed the issue as less of a priority and were willing to bend on it. The debate also posed broader issues involving the fight for women's emancipation and its connection to the working-class fight for socialism.

3. IMMIGRATION

In recent years, tens of millions of people have been forced to emigrate, either driven by economic necessity caused by the workings of imperialism or as refugees of war. At the same time, massive campaigns against immigrants and immigration have occurred throughout the United States and Europe in particular. Anti-immigrant moves by capitalist governments have also helped spawn racist and xenophobic movements, leading to deadly attacks on immigrants and their defenders. In response, supporters of immigrant rights confront important questions: What is the cause of immigration? What stance should socialists take? What is the possibility for building alliances between native-born and immigrant workers?

The Second International took up similar issues at its congresses of 1904 and 1907. The exchanges at these gatherings pitted a minority advocating immigration restrictions against the majority of delegates who opposed such restrictions and viewed immigrants as fellow workers to be supported and welcomed into the struggle.

4. IMPERIALISM AND COLONIALISM

By the early twentieth century, the world had been divided into a handful of imperialist powers holding colonial empires and a majority of the world's population oppressed under the colonial yoke. Outwardly, the situation looks somewhat different today. Yet, this same basic division of the world remains present, as evidenced in the prevalence across Africa, Asia, and Latin America of hunger, poverty, and limits to health care access, as well as the differential effects of climate change. Socialists in the twenty-first century thus continue to face questions about the nature of imperialism, its effect on working people in both oppressed and oppressor nations, and how it can be fought.

At the time of the Second International congresses of 1904 and 1907, virtually all of Africa and much of Asia consisted of colonial possessions. Debates at these congresses pitted advocates of "socialist colonialism" against those condemning the colonial system in its entirety, as well as counterposing delegates who scorned and ridiculed subjects of colonial rule to those who defended their interests.

5. SOCIALIST TACTICS FOR ACHIEVING POWER

The growing sympathy with socialism in the United States in recent years has led to electoral victories by a number of self-professed socialist candidates for US Congress and local office. Such electoral gains have provoked debates among socialists over strategy and tactics in the struggle to win power: How will socialist power be won? Should socialists enter capitalist administrations as junior partners? Should socialists support or participate in bourgeois parties?

In 1900 and 1904, congresses of the Second International debated the question of socialist participation in government in relation to the Millerand affair referred to earlier. Involved in these verbal exchanges were supporters and opponents of accepting ministerial positions in capitalist governments. Some delegates also expressed the view that doing so was simply a tactical decision to be made by parties in each country.

The debate on Millerandism posed what many activists today have been grappling with: What should be socialists' objective for advancing working-class interests? What is the relationship between reform and revolution?

Legacy and Continuity

In today's world, working people and youth confront numerous issues that will require prolonged battles in the coming years—struggles over climate change and its consequences, imperialist wars and militarization, abortion and women's rights, racist police killings, health care, labor battles and antiworker assaults, threats from ultrarightist and fascist forces, and more.

These struggles will pose both opportunities and challenges for socialists and all fighters for social change: How can these battles be waged most effectively? What must be done to maximize chances of success? To answer these questions, a study of socialist legacy and continuity can be of major benefit.

The Second International of 1889 to 1914 obviously cannot offer a guidebook for the present. Nevertheless, properly examined in context, the experience of socialists a century ago can provide valuable lessons and examples.

Today a new generation of young people and others are being won to socialism, having seen the dead end of capitalism and the threats it poses to human existence. Many have decided to join the struggle for social justice and a better world. By studying the Second International's tradition and legacy—without overlooking its contradictions and weaknesses—those coming to socialism today can help find their place within the movement's proud history and join in the fight for a revolutionary transformation of society.

About This Edition

This is a book of debates that occurred at four Second International congresses.

Oral debates have one important advantage in comparison to written exchanges: there's less of a tendency of speakers to sand down the rough edges of their words, or to come up with carefully crafted formulations to justify positions and make them palatable. Some points raised in these verbal duels would almost certainly not have been put down on paper. Such candidness can be a window into the underlying issues driving the debates.

Featured in this book's exchanges are key historic figures in the Second International: August Bebel, Karl Kautsky, Eduard Bernstein, Rosa Luxemburg, Victor Adler, Jules Guesde, Jean Jaurès, Émile Vandervelde, Édouard Vaillant, Georgy Plekhanov, Georg Ledebour, and Hendrick van Kol. Participants also included several individuals who went on to play important roles in the Communist International after 1919, such as Clara Zetkin, Christian Rakovsky, and Karl Radek. By observing how the Second International's leading figures participated in these debates, readers can better understand the positions adopted by these individuals after 1914. It likewise helps open the door to continued study of the parties within the International that these individuals represented.

The five issues under debate in this book were far from the only topics of contention in the Second International. Debates also took place over the general strike, May Day, the role of trade unions, cooperatives, party unity, and numerous other issues. The issues featured in this book were chosen because of their similarity to questions under discussion today. The excerpts from the debates included here have been selected so as to bring out as clearly as possible the political differences expressed.

As for the time period, the years 1900 to 1910 were selected because this period saw the emergence of the trends within the Second International that crystallized fully after 1914. The debates at the 1900,

1904, 1907, and 1910 international congresses thus foreshadow the subsequent division of the world socialist movement.

Each chapter contains an introductory note describing the background and circumstances of the particular debate, the resolutions under discussion, and the oral exchange itself. The text of the resolutions are taken from *Under the Socialist Banner*. Oral debates are translated from the French and German editions of the congress proceedings. A list of these official records can be found at the end of this volume. When going through these oral debates, readers should keep in mind that some of the language in these exchanges from over a century ago would not be used or accepted today.

Two articles by V. I. Lenin have been included as an appendix, presenting his view of the trends within the Second International. Endnotes, together with a glossary of names, organizations, and publications, have been provided to give the necessary background to readers, enabling them to more easily follow the debate.

I would like to acknowledge help and support from Daniel Gaido, Peter Hudis, Paul LeBlanc, Ben Lewis, John McDonald, Anne McShane, John Riddell, Nancy Rosenstock, Graham Seaman, Bob Schwarz, and Lyndon White.

Mike Taber
September 2022

1.

The Debate on Socialist Participation in Government (Millerandism)

Introductory Note on the Millerandism Debate

At the heart of the debate around socialist participation in capitalist governments was the issue of the movement's strategic objective: was it to be reform or revolution?

Such an alternative confronted the Second International at its birth. The founding congress in 1889, organized in close collaboration with Frederick Engels, faced a competing labor congress held in the very same city at the very same time. The rival gathering was organized by reformist forces in France known as the Possibilists—named as such due to their overriding goal of achieving reforms they felt were possible under capitalism.

In distinction to the Possibilists, the Second International from its birth adopted an openly revolutionary perspective. As reviewed in the introduction to this book, a resolution adopted at its founding congress declared "that the emancipation of labor and humanity cannot occur without the international action of the proletariat—organized in class-based parties—which seizes political power through the expropriation of the capitalist class and the social appropriation of the means of production."

While reformist currents were present at the Second International's first several congresses, these currents did not openly attempt to question the movement's adopted revolutionary outlook.

The first major challenge to this perspective came from Eduard Bernstein, a follower and collaborator of Karl Marx and Frederick Engels when both were alive. In the late 1890s, however, Bernstein became increasingly critical of Marxism's political conclusions; these criticisms were codified in his 1899 book, *Evolutionary Socialism.* In that book Bernstein openly rejected the revolutionary goals of the socialist movement, asserting that "the ultimate aim of socialism is nothing, but the movement is everything."[1] Bernstein further expressed the view that revolution was no longer a strategic necessity and that capitalism had acquired the potential to overcome the contradictions and crises pointed to by Marx and Engels. The perspective Bernstein outlined came to be known within the socialist movement as "revisionism."

Bernstein's challenge found an echo in some sectors of the world socialist movement, giving rise to sharp polemics and debates, as many prominent socialists forcefully defended Marxism's revolutionary foundations. In October 1899, a congress of the German Social Democratic Party (SPD) formally condemned Bernstein's views by a vote of 216 to 21. The lopsidedness of that vote, however, did not reflect the real support for Bernstein's views within the German party. Indeed, many members and officials supported some of his conclusions but were reluctant to express those opinions openly.

The second controversy—and the immediate cause of the debate recorded in this chapter—involved Alexandre Millerand, a member of the Independent Socialist group in the French parliament. In June 1899 Millerand accepted a position in the capitalist government of France as minister of commerce.

Up until that time, the question of socialist participation in government had not been posed in any significant way. In the movement's early years, socialists were often isolated and persecuted—a situation that provided little motivation for procapitalist forces to draw them into government. But as the socialist and labor movements grew, some liberal and radical bourgeois currents began to reach out to them, in a bid to attract working-class backing. In exchange, however, socialists were expected to give political support to these capitalist politicians.

In 1894, five years before Millerand's entry into government, Engels warned of such dangers:

> After the common victory we might perhaps be offered some *seats in the new Government*—but always in a *minority. Here lies the greatest danger.* After the February Revolution in 1848 the French socialistic Democrats (the *Réforme* people, Ledru-Rollin, Louis Blanc, Flocon, etc.) were incautious enough to accept such positions. As a minority in the Government they involuntarily bore the responsibility for all the infamy and treachery which the majority, composed of pure Republicans,

> committed against the working class, while at the same time their participation in the government completely paralysed the revolutionary action of the working class they were supposed to represent.[2]

The "Millerand affair" of 1899 led to a wide-ranging discussion in the working-class movement, giving rise to the main debates at the 1900 and 1904 Second International congresses.

At the Paris Congress of 1900, the principal resolution on the question was drafted by Karl Kautsky, the Second International's leading theoretician, who was known as a defender of orthodox Marxism. Yet Kautsky's resolution, while condemning socialist participation in capitalist governments under "normal" circumstances, nevertheless left the door open to it under "exceptional" ones. "If in some special instance the political situation necessitates this dangerous expedient," Kautsky's resolution stated, "that is a question of tactics and not of principle." The aim of Kautsky in making this motion, as he subsequently stated, was to defend a revolutionary perspective while seeking socialist unity. It was intended as a compromise.

Counterposed to the Kautsky resolution at the Paris Congress was one put forward by Enrico Ferri and Jules Guesde, opposing socialist participation in capitalist government ministries under all circumstances. A long debate on this question took place in a commission and at the congress plenary. At the debate's conclusion, the Kautsky resolution was adopted, receiving 29 votes against 9 for that of Guesde and Ferri.

Nevertheless, the ambiguity of the Kautsky resolution—humorously labeled the "rubber resolution," owing to its pliability—and the dissatisfaction it engendered meant that the question would inevitably come up again.

At its 1903 congress in Dresden, the German SPD adopted a resolution, drafted by Kautsky and August Bebel, unambiguously condemning all socialist participation in capitalist governments, with no provisions for "exceptional circumstances."

Seeing the SPD's 1903 resolution as a way to reverse the Kautsky resolution adopted at the Second International's 1900 congress, the French Workers Party, led by Guesde, submitted this resolution to the 1904 Second International congress in Amsterdam. It therefore became known as the Dresden-Amsterdam resolution.

Opposed to this resolution was one presented by Victor Adler and Émile Vandervelde. Endorsing the ambiguities of the Kautsky resolution four years earlier, the Adler-Vandervelde resolution asserted "[t]hat the Social Democracy, in regard of the dangers and the inconveniences of the participation in the government in bourgeois society, brings to mind and confirms the Kautsky resolution, passed at the International Congress of Paris in 1900."

Many supporters of the Adler-Vandervelde position argued that while they agreed with the Dresden-Amsterdam resolution in its condemnation of ministerialism, the issue of tactics should be left to each party. Some also accused Dresden-Amsterdam supporters of attempting to issue condemnations and excommunications of individuals and parties.

In the congress commission taking up the question, the Adler-Vandervelde resolution was rejected by a vote of 24 to 16. But when the question reached the congress plenary, the vote was considerably closer; the Adler-Vandervelde resolution failed, but only by a tie vote of 21 to 21. The Dresden-Amsterdam resolution was then adopted by a vote of 25 to 5, with 12 abstentions.

While the Dresden-Amsterdam resolution did not specifically criticize the 1900 resolution, it annulled a major piece of the earlier document by eliminating its "exceptional circumstances" clause. However, the closeness of the congress vote indicated the growing strength of opportunist forces within the Second International.

Alongside the rejection of socialist acceptance of ministerial positions in capitalist governments, the Amsterdam Congress reiterated the movement's support for independent working-class political action and its rejection of support for capitalist political parties, stating that it "condemns any attempt made to veil the ever-growing class antagonism, for the purpose of facilitating an understanding with bourgeois parties." That perspective was in line with Kautsky's assessment of "the bankruptcy of all capitalist parties."[3]

The policy adopted at the 1904 congress would be generally followed by the socialist movement over the next decade. At the start of the First World War in 1914, however, this policy was thrown out the window like many others. Numerous Second International and Socialist Party leaders—including some who had most strenuously opposed Millerand, such as Guesde—accepted ministerial posts in wartime governments.

The Millerandism Debate at the 1900 Paris Congress

Proposed Resolutions

Kautsky Resolution (Adopted)

I

In a modern democratic state the conquest of political power by the proletariat cannot be effected by a *coup de main*, but must be the result of a long and toilsome work of proletarian organization, political and economic, of the physical and moral regeneration of the working class, and of the gradual conquest of municipal and legislative assemblies.

But in a country where governmental power is centralized, it cannot be conquered in a fragmentary manner.

The entry of an isolated socialist into a bourgeois government cannot be regarded as the normal commencement of the conquest of political power, but only as a compulsory expedient, transitory and exceptional.

If in some special instance the political situation necessitates this dangerous expedient, that is a question of tactics and not of principle; the International Congress is not called upon to pronounce on that point. But in any case, the entry of a socialist into a bourgeois government affords no hope of good results for the militant proletariat unless the great majority of the Socialist Party approves of this step and the socialist minister remains the delegate of his party.

In the contrary case, in which such a minister becomes independent of the party or represents only a section of it, his intervention in a bourgeois ministry threatens disorganization and confusion to the militant proletariat, threatens to weaken rather than to strengthen it, and hinders rather than advances the proletarian conquest of public powers.

In any case, the Congress is of the opinion that, even in the most exceptional circumstances, a socialist ought to quit the ministry whenever the latter gives any proof of partiality in the struggle between capital and labor. No minister delegated by the Socialist Party can continue to participate in the government if the party concludes that this government has not observed absolute impartiality in the relations between capital and labor.

II

The Congress reasserts that the class struggle forbids all alliances with any fraction whatever of the capitalist class.

Even admitting that exceptional circumstances may sometimes render coalitions necessary (without confusion of party or tactics), these coalitions, which the party should seek to reduce to the smallest possible number until they entirely disappear, must not be permitted except insofar as their necessity is recognized by the district or national organization to which the groups concerned belong.

Guesde-Ferri Resolution

The Fifth International Congress, meeting in Paris, declares again that the conquest of public power refers to the political expropriation of the capitalist class, whether this expropriation takes place peacefully or violently.

As a result, under the capitalist system, it allows only for the occupation of elected positions that the [Socialist] Party can capture by means of its own forces, that is, workers organized in a class party. It thereby prohibits any socialist participation in bourgeois governments, against which socialists must remain in irreconcilable opposition.

Plenary Debate

Émile Vandervelde (Belgium, reporter): . . . Without pretending to reflect the views of all the commission's members, I'll give my personal opinion.

With regard to alliances and coalitions with bourgeois parties, I can be extremely brief. That can be done only with the greatest caution, given that they can weaken the proletariat's class consciousness. But let us not forget that coalitions are sometimes a necessary evil. . . .

Whatever the intellectual and moral value of having a socialist minister, we believe that the disadvantages are infinitely greater than the advantages. I would say that Millerand and his friends have committed an error in accepting such an appointment on his own personal responsibility. [*Applause from the French Workers Party*] And they have committed an even greater error in remaining there contrary to the view of an important section of French socialism. . . .

Our difference with the French Workers Party is that we believe the ministerial question to be one of tactics and not of principle. . . .

Enrico Ferri (Italy): . . . It is said that one must distinguish tactics from theory. I say that one cannot make such a scholastic distinction, since practice is simply theory in action, and theory is simply generalized practice. You cannot open a window after closing the door. These are the rubbery edges that you propose. I travel through Italy a lot, and I'm always seeing comrades declaring there to be exceptional conditions that require abandoning principles.

The Kautsky resolution proclaims all the principles nicely, but it says that the congress should not concern itself with tactical details. That is wrong: one cannot separate tactics from principles. Is it possible to go forward while freely allowing a socialist minister to put principles in the background? . . .

We believe that the Kautsky motion contains more dangers than its author realizes. It is a slope in which the beginning is known, but not where it ends. . . .

Jean Jaurès (France): In order to defend liberty and obtain universal suffrage, all socialist parties practice alliances. During the Dreyfus affair, almost all socialist parties in the world declared they would have failed to do their duty had they left the battle against the organized lie to the liberal bourgeoisie. . . .[4]

On the other more controversial question of participation in bourgeois governments, I support the Kautsky motion because it expresses a balance. Its view is a bit unstable, but it is the only one acceptable today.

Vandervelde said that the Millerand question is a purely French one, that it's posed only in France. Let me express my regret that it's not posed elsewhere. . . . It could have been posed in Belgium during the last elections, had the Belgian socialists and liberals beaten the clerical majority. But Vandervelde's question will not have come up, because the Socialist Party will not leave the responsibility to individuals. The question will be posed in an impersonal form.

I support the Kautsky motion because it leaves to the judgment of the Socialist Party how to decide the issue in each specific situation. It also affirms that what's involved is a practical question, and not one of theory or principle. . . .

Jules Guesde (France): . . . I turn to the Kautsky resolution. I am with Kautsky when he reminds us that the entrance of a socialist minister into government cannot be considered as the start of the conquest of political power. In this way he distinguishes the taking of power by the working class from ministerial begging. [*Applause from the French Workers Party*]

I am also with Kautsky when he reminds us that in order to carry out our program, the entirety of central power is necessary. Without that there can only be ineffectual reforms and not the replacement of the capitalist system by a collectivist system. He does not challenge the necessity of a class dictatorship as a final goal—a measure before which the bourgeoisie of 1793 did not shrink. [*Protests by part of the French section; applause*]

Kautsky is also correct when he denounces the confusion and disorganization introduced into proletarian ranks by the participation of a socialist in government, and when he says that such participation, far from getting us nearer to our goal, moves us further away from it. Additionally, he is correct that instead of being a source of strength, such participation would be a source of weakness for our party.

Such a focus is all the more important given that the failures are not just national. Ferri noted that such failures are happening all over. The backbone of the international workers' party is starting to bend. Our actions have gained in quantity, but have lost in quality.

I nearly voted for the Kautsky motion, because it contains an essential initial correction. But the organizations I represent cannot agree with Kautsky when he condemns the "new fact" theoretically but then accepts it in the future as an accidental occurrence. But the class struggle, accidentally or not, must not lead to class collaboration, as the accident would risk becoming fatal.

A socialist who enters a bourgeois ministry, Liebknecht said, might still believe himself to be a socialist, but he would cease to be so.[5] Because a person cannot serve two masters at the same time, a person cannot serve two classes.

In short, one cannot be both an agent of social conservation and of social revolution. There is a contradiction, an incompatibility that cannot be erased, that cannot be eliminated—even with the eventual authorization given by the party. Far from remedying the evil, that would only aggravate it. . . .

Édouard Vaillant (France): . . . I ask Kautsky why, after fighting victoriously against Bernstein in Germany, does he capitulate now?[6] [*Protests*] Our decision must be clear, and the Kautsky resolution is not. The congress needs to take a formal and precise decision: to vote in favor of the text of the resolution proposed by the commission minority [the Guesde-Ferri resolution]. That you cannot refuse to do. [*Applause from one side of the hall*]

Ignaz Auer (Germany): . . . I voted [in the commission] in favor of the Kautsky resolution. I did not do so because I agree with all of its terms, but I support its general tendency. One can criticize it for being vague and ambiguous, or that it does not contain prescriptions for every case. But if it was that complete, I would not vote for it. We do not want to tie our hands for all things that might come up. We want a resolution that, while remaining true to our theories and our program, is appropriate for the situation at hand. We do not renounce our right. We are not fanatics, prophets, church founders, or people with the ultimate truth in our pocket. [*Lively applause*] We seek the truth, and in pursuit of this truth we must keep our road clear. [*Applause*] That is why we vote for the Kautsky resolution. . . .

The Millerandism Debate at the 1904 Amsterdam Congress

Proposed Resolutions

Dresden-Amsterdam Resolution (Adopted)

The Congress condemns most energetically the revisionist attempts, in the direction of changing our tried and victorious tactics based on the class struggle, and of replacing the conquest of the public powers through the supreme struggle with the bourgeoisie with a policy of concession to the established order.

The consequence of such revisionist tactics would be to change us from a party seeking the swiftest possible transformation of bourgeois society into socialist society—from a party strictly revolutionary in the best sense of the word—into a party contenting itself with the reform of bourgeois society.

Therefore the Congress, convinced, contrary to the present revisionist tendencies, that class antagonisms, far from diminishing, are intensifying, declares:

1. That the party disclaims any responsibility whatever for the political and economic conditions based on capitalist production, and consequently could not approve any methods tending to maintain the ruling class in power.

2. That the Social Democracy could accept no share in the government within capitalist society, as was definitely declared by the Kautsky resolution adopted by the international congress of Paris in 1900.

The Congress moreover condemns any attempt made to veil the ever-growing class antagonism, for the purpose of facilitating an understanding with bourgeois parties.

The Congress looks to the socialist parliamentary group to avail itself of its increased power—increased both by the greater number of its members and by the substantial growth of the body of electors behind it—to persevere in its propaganda toward the final goal of socialism, and, in conformity with our program, to defend most resolutely the interests of the working class, the extension and consolidation of its political liberties, to demand equality of rights for all; to continue with more energy than ever the struggle against militarism, against the colonial and imperialistic policy, against all manner of injustice, slavery, and exploitation; and, finally, to set itself energetically to improve social legislation to make it possible for the working class to accomplish its political and civilizing mission.

Adler-Vandervelde Resolution

The Congress affirms in the most strenuous way the necessity of maintaining unwaveringly our tried and glorious tactics based on the class war and shall never allow that the conquest of the political power in the teeth of the bourgeoisie shall be replaced by a policy of concession to the established order.

The result of this policy of concession would be to change a party that pursues the swiftest possible transformation of bourgeois society into a socialist society—consequently revolutionary in the best sense of the word—into a party that contents itself with reforming bourgeois society.

For this reason, the Congress, persuaded that class antagonisms, far from diminishing, increase continually, states:

1. That the party declines all responsibility whatsoever for the political and economic conditions based on capitalist production and consequently cannot approve of any means that tend to maintain in power the dominant class.

2. That the Social Democracy, in regard to the dangers and the inconveniences of the participation in the government in bourgeois society, brings to mind and confirms the Kautsky resolution, passed at the International Congress of Paris in 1900.

Commission Debate

Jean Jaurès (France): . . . It is the duty of international socialism to define principles and to specify the methods for implementing them. International socialism did so when it proclaimed the need to win governmental power. But when it comes to each nation's tactics, the question is more complex and needs to be approached carefully. Socialism aims to emancipate the working class in all countries, whether under autocratic, constitutional, or republican regimes. We should therefore avoid prescribing inflexible or uniform rules. . . .

It is said that we are altering our principles. Class collaboration is spoken of. We believe that there is an essential antagonism between the classes, an irreducible antagonism, stemming from conflicting property modes. But if, profiting from the republican regime, we believe that the interests of our beliefs and our proletariat compel us to assist the republican bourgeoisie to resolve questions such as the secularization of instruction in state schools, we would not at all be betraying the principle of the class struggle. The interest of the proletariat is our chief law. We are guided by the principles of the class struggle and the interests of the proletariat. We do not in the least betray these principles, any more than German Social Democracy betrayed them on the day that it, along with Bebel, recognized the need to participate in elections to the Landtag [state assembly].[7] . . .

In 1900, the Kautsky resolution, which we accepted, was approved by the Paris Congress. It declared that participation [in government ministries] was dangerous and should not be accidental. Instead, it recognized that it was possible under the control of the national [party] congress. Did the Dresden resolution radically modify the Kautsky resolution? The latter resolution prohibited the socialist proletariat from *seeking* participation, while the Dresden resolution spoke of not *accepting* it. Is this a formula worthy of a great international party like ours? If a time came when it might be useful to accept socialist participation, we should not be ashamed of it. An hour may also come when it might also be in the interest of the proletariat to seek it. . . .

Karl Kautsky (Germany): The motion to make the Dresden Congress resolution into a general tactical guideline for international socialism does not come from the German Social Democrats. But when other nations want to present it as such, we can only greet this joyfully.

We can only agree with this if it does not contain an exaggeration of the original text. Such an exaggeration—albeit unintentional—has crept in, making the resolution say we refused to *accept* a share of governmental power, while the original only refuses to *seek* it. Jaurès has already paid attention to this discrepancy, but there is no difficulty here. Because the applicants are ready to accept the exact translation of the German text. Of course, Jaurès thinks that there is a factual difference between the two types of reading, because if I am ready to accept an office, I must also have the courage to strive for it. He thinks that the German text is therefore only more timid than the French. But he is wrong. The passage concerned is based on the Paris resolution [of 1900] that bears my name. There it is expressly stated, however, that a socialist may enter a bourgeois government only in difficult situations. I had in mind the situation in France after September 4, 1870, when socialists debated whether Blanqui or Delescluze should join the government with the purpose of organizing the country's defense.[8] But the resolution explicitly says that the rare event of a socialist assuming office has dangers for Social Democracy, but is a sacrifice that sometimes cannot be avoided. The distinction between *striving for* and *accepting* is therefore not a tangential difference but an essential one.

Here in Amsterdam, the question that we have to decide is different from the one taken up in Paris. No longer is it a question of whether a socialist may enter a bourgeois government and under what circumstances. The question now is what are our chosen tactics and what do we seek. And here we absolutely declare that our efforts should not be aimed at gaining a share in a bourgeois government.

Now, of course, it is being declared that such a rule cannot be established internationally, that tactics are a purely national matter, into which one should not interfere. But those who are now issuing this principle violated it themselves when they voted without hesitation in Paris for the resolution we presented, which lays down tactical rules just as in the Dresden resolution.

Jaurès thinks that the international congress should then also have the right to decide on participation in elections to the Prussian Landtag. But a distinction must be made between tactical principles and their application. . . . Jaurès referred to the Prussian state elections to show how changeable tactics are and how difficult it is to lay down general rules for them. But here too the same distinction applies between a principle and its application.

The way in which tactical principles are applied changes continuously with changing situations, but tactical principles themselves remain the same. The question of participation in elections to the Prussian Landtag did not mean abolishing our previous tactical principles, but was the result of a calculation as to whether we were strong enough to win mandates under the three-class voting system.[9] The tactical principles of the Dresden resolution were still valid in the Prussian Landtag elections. German Social Democracy has followed these principles unchanged for a generation, and it is precisely this that we see as a guarantee for our principles. These principles hold similarly in other capitalist countries and can lead Social Democracy there to the same victories that it led to for us.

Jaurès sees these principles only as an inhibition that prevents him from fighting reaction together with bourgeois capitalism, in accordance with the specific situation in France. But our Dresden principles have not prevented German Social Democracy from acting in similar ways. Even the Communist Manifesto declares that Communists support the radical bourgeoisie and bourgeois democracy against reactionary forces wherever we are able to do so, such as in runoff elections.[10]

But we do not support bourgeois democracy under all circumstances. Jaurès and his friends count among the revolutionary bourgeoisie to be supported elements such as Galliffet[11] and even the king of Italy. And they support the liberal bourgeoisie even when it associates with Russian absolutism. It is the government supported by Jaurès and his friends that is partly responsible for the fact that the bloodhounds of Kishinev are still in power today.[12]

If our resolution can prevent deviations such as those indicated above, it would be a great gain, in my opinion. It would also be a gain for Jaurès himself, preventing him from pursuing a policy that drives him away from us. If the Dresden resolution gains international validity, it will create the basis for a unification of the two factions of French socialism and thus becomes a powerful means of promoting and revitalizing the proletarian mass struggle.[13] I therefore ask you to adopt our resolution.

Daniel De Leon (United States): The argument of Jaurès is correct: an international congress has the right to decide questions of principle but not questions of method. But Kautsky is right to object that Jaurès subscribed to such a decision at the Paris Congress. At the same time, however, Kautsky demonstrated that the Dresden resolution goes beyond the Kautsky resolution of the Paris Congress.

The international congress must decide on questions of principle and not of method; the latter relates to the needs of the place and the moment. Kautsky reproaches Jaurès for having collaborated with Galliffet. He says that in 1900 he had in mind only exceptional cases of wars of invasion. But in 1900 Millerand was in power. That is why we are delighted with the vote on the Kautsky resolution. In America, the question you are discussing does not arise; there is no danger of confusion with the bourgeoisie in the United States.

The Kautsky resolution [of 1900] should be rejected. . . . It has correctly been called the "rubber resolution." [*Laughter*] . . .

Victor Adler (Austria): Most of the delegates, including Jaurès, want the congress to determine the foundations of the struggle for the emancipation of the working class. The difficulty is not determining the rules of the class struggle, but applying these rules. We are not fighting in a dream but in reality; and realities vary according to country.

I am not saying that we *should not* prescribe international rules of socialist method; I am saying that we *cannot* do so. Nobody would be firmer than me if it were possible to provide a rule applicable for all doubtful cases. But tactics depend on circumstances.

Four years ago the Kautsky resolution dealt with the Millerand affair that was then posed. But after the Paris Congress, the question was not done away with; it remains on the agenda. Isn't this proof that the Kautsky resolution did not resolve the question?

The situation has changed in France. It's not a question of personal participation in a bourgeois government, but of participation by an entire party in parliament, within a political bloc.[14] Today the situation is more serious; the responsibility is heavier.

In all sincerity I believe that the tactics of Jaurès are false and dangerous, but I do not want the congress to condemn them. I say to the French comrades: I doubt the justice and soundness of your tactics, but I don't venture to condemn them. The Dresden resolution is an excellent declaration of principles, which cannot be stated any more sharply. But the international congress must not pronounce condemnations that can be revised only every three or four years. We must insist on a positive declaration of the class-struggle standpoint, and we warn the international proletariat against abandoning this path. But we should not brand the minority or put a curse on them.

Émile Vandervelde (Belgium): I will be brief, as my friend Adler said most of what I was going to say.

No one, including Jaurès, spoke against the Dresden resolution. The essence of this resolution is, fundamentally, the class struggle. And that's why we oppose those in France who have advocated class collaboration. Those who defend that have abandoned socialism.

Given our agreement on principles, can we be in agreement with their application in each country? Surely we will not presume to ignore variations in temperament, milieu, tradition, and national needs. It is inadmissible for the congress to act as judge and arbiter on questions of national tactics. And Guesde is in agreement with me, because he said that his aim is to reaffirm the fundamental principles of socialism. That solemn affirmation is useful and necessary, and no one among us will dispute it. The German resolution, drafted for Germany, would need a few amendments to be adapted to the needs of an international congress.

The Kautsky resolution [of 1900] did not imply a prohibition of all socialist participation in government. The Paris resolution of 1899 is clearer than the Dresden resolution.[15] If it's necessary to come back to this point, why not simply reissue the Kautsky formula? We examined the whole question in 1900. At that time we proclaimed that it is not possible to absolutely close all doors.

With regard to reformist tendencies, I still consider them dangerous for socialism, a policy that supports a bourgeois government at some point becoming its official organ.

In agreement with Adler, I refuse to issue condemnations and promulgate excommunications. On behalf of the Belgian delegation, I ask that we adopt the essence of the Dresden resolution, confining it to affirmations without any condemnations. Condemnations weaken and divide us. Affirmations bring us solidarity and make us stronger in our common struggle against capitalism.

Enrico Ferri (Italy): In 1900 I was the reporter in Paris against the Kautsky resolution, which dealt only with specific cases, while I was defending a general method. So at Amsterdam I am being consistent in voting for the Dresden resolution. The formula is not perfect, as amendments would take too much time. But I will vote for it, interpreting the Italian socialist consciousness, formulated at its congress in Bologna.[16]

I join with Vandervelde and Adler in excluding any spirit of stigma and excommunication against any individual or current. No one is infallible. The congress will not pronounce any excommunications.

I also say that there is a tendency to make too absolute distinctions between principles and tactics. In his admirable speech, Jaurès affirmed the unity of our principles, but he doubts that an international congress is able in practice to set socialist tactics adapted to every nation.

When one goes on a trip, a compass and a map are necessary. One has to determine the point of departure and the point of arrival. From a fixed point of departure, one must determine the point of arrival. While making allowance for vicissitudes and the exact course, this must all be subordinated to the perspective of reaching the arrival point. Do not separate principles and tactics. If one sticks too much to principles, action risks becoming futile. But if, in carrying out tasks one forgets principles, then we lose the route indicated by the compass and the working masses become disoriented. So tactics must proceed from principles.

The Kautsky resolution does not authorize socialist participation except in exceptional and temporary cases, and it explains that whatever tendencies there might be in bourgeois parties, the capitalist bloc remains untouched, with the aim of maintaining the system of private property.

Let us help liberal parties give the coup de grâce to feudal remnants. Fine. There should be an end to systematic confusion between socialist action and that of the bourgeoisie, since the democratic party of the bourgeoisie today will become reactionary tomorrow, while socialist action will want to continue. Here we see the danger of deviating from the compass of principles and then having socialist action absorbed by parliamentary action, which is only superficial. Then there is no more socialist action, but simply a parliamentary contest between supporters and opponents of ministries. It is this danger that we are on guard against in Italy with the Giolitti cabinet.[17] Our compass is the principle of the class struggle!

The difference between class struggle and class collaboration is measured in nuance and tact. It is a question of tactics.

At the beginning I did not begrudge my admiration for Jaurès, and I restate it. But I warn him that with his tactic of participation he may well carry out a very good reformist policy but a very bad socialist policy. The

Amsterdam Congress should proclaim that socialism must be based on the main road of the class struggle, with our socialist ideal on the horizon.

Engels once wrote that within socialist parties there is always a right wing and a left wing. These nuances are natural and legitimate. With these different points of view, unity is maintained in every party. Questions are seen in their true proletarian aspect, based on working-class interests. Without party unity, we come to see only the extreme and dangerous aspects of questions. For this reason I appeal here to socialism's national and international unity.

Georgy Plekhanov (Russia): . . . It is not enough to be in agreement on an ideal. It is necessary to be in agreement regarding the means of action; otherwise the socialist ideal is compromised in the eyes of the proletariat. I do not understand why Adler refuses to condemn a tendency that he proclaims to be false and erroneous. One must not refuse to condemn bad tendencies in order to spare individuals. . . .

The Vandervelde-Adler resolution lacks clarity. The Dresden resolution is clearer and more precise. The vote on this resolution will alarm the clerical and reactionary enemy more than any other act by the international congress. It's important to increase the scope of the resolution approved in Paris in 1900, which does not at all contradict the experience of the last four years.

Christian Rakovsky (Bulgaria): . . . You [Jaurès] formed a bloc with the Radical Party. Socialism [in France] has come to be a postulate relegated to program and principles, while socialist activity in the country is subsumed in parliamentary action. Will you resume socialist propaganda after clericalism is defeated? Afterward will there not be another reactionary force to combat? You go from class collaboration on an exceptional basis to permanent collaboration. Would we not then wind up modifying the purity of our principles, of the socialist conception? *L'Humanité* invokes for each country the great principles of 1789. That's not enough for us! That's not where the principle of the class struggle comes from.

The Vandervelde-Adler resolution lacks precision. We ask of you tactical rules and not old declarations of principle that we are all in agreement with.

No ambiguity! After the Paris Congress, Jaurès said that the Kautsky resolution was a victory for his tendency. [*Jaurès protests.*] It should be noted that the Kautsky motion was the result of a compromise. Socialist unity is not desirable if it impedes socialist action. One must have the courage to face reality.

We desire immediate practical results. Without socialism in Germany, the liberal bourgeoisie would be more liberal, and legislation would be more reformist.

If we are to stand in the way of immediate reforms, so be it! It is sometimes inevitable. Because we do not work for today nor for tomorrow; international socialism works for the future.

August Bebel (Germany): . . . The [Dresden] resolution before us does nothing more than establish the tactics of Social Democracy in the various countries within the limits that are given by the character of the state in question. Differences of opinion cannot be ruled out. Such differences in parties will always exist. What is necessary, however, is the unity and cohesion of Social Democracy in each country, which is possible only if we stand not just on the same principles, but also on the same tactical grounds on all questions of general politics. . . .

We believe that the tactics that we in Germany have adopted against bourgeois parties and governments can and should also be used in France and other countries. We do not demand that any valuable concessions to the working class, wherever they come from, should be rejected. We have always accepted what we thought was genuinely positive, regardless of whether it was offered by the government or by one of the bourgeois parties. But that did not prevent us from fighting the government or these parties with the most decisive and ruthless measures as soon as they took actions that we regarded as pernicious. We have always retained our full freedom and independence, bearing in mind the fact that we have a state against us based on class rule.

But the party that Comrade Jaurès represents in France is in a formal alliance with the government and the bourgeois parties behind it, which are united in the so-called [Left] Bloc. That fact forces these comrades to refrain from many things they should be demanding in the interests of the working class and to deny many things that they should be fighting against under all circumstances. Such a position creates confusion in our ranks. The energetic elements are disoriented; they see that such tactics result in serious damage to the interests of the proletariat. The result is to drive our best forces toward anarchism; at the same time, many dubious bourgeois elements enter the party. Jaurès's tactics do not drive the bourgeois parties to the left, but rather force socialists to the right. . . .

Jaurès says that because France is a republic and Germany is a reactionary-ruled monarchy, the Dresden resolution therefore does not fit France. Certainly we [in Germany] have monarchies, and we are governed in a most reactionary manner. My dear Jaurès! We envy France for its republic and, even more, for its universal suffrage in elections to all representative bodies. But, as has often happened in important strikes in France in recent years, your republic did not prevent both the police and the military from being called out against strikers. That is, the republican government took sides against the workers and for the bourgeoisie in all of these cases.

The republic is also a class state, but it has an advantage [for the bourgeoisie] over a monarchy in that the class struggle takes place in a far more undercover way. Our police and judiciary [in Germany] have not failed to use violence against the workers, but the military has not been deployed against strikers since the great miners' strike of 1889. That occurs not just in France, but also in republican Switzerland and in the great republic across the ocean, the United States. In Switzerland the militia is deployed in every major strike, and the militias in the rural districts are used against the industrial workers, as Comrade Moor told us. In the United States I only need to recall the unheard-of events of recent times in Colorado, Pennsylvania, Pittsburgh, and so on. No monarchical public prosecutor could act in a more brutal way against the workers.

Where does this different treatment between monarchy and republic come from? For better or worse, monarchies sometimes have to maintain their prestige a little. They also need the workers against the bourgeoisie, as happened under Bismarck. They have to give the impression that they stand above parties, as happened in Germany, by enacting so-called social legislation—our opinion of which was always correct.[18] For the republic, on the other hand, the government is the unmistakable representative of the ruling classes, whose interests it protects.

It's therefore also a big mistake to interpret the acceptance of one or more socialists into government as an acceptance of socialism. Our opponents know very well that the capitalist class will not become friends of the socialists, but that some socialists will become friends of the capitalist class and that the socialist representatives in the cabinet will be forced to take responsibility for all actions of a bourgeois government. . . .

Our point of view is that we vote for all measures that are of benefit to the working class and resolutely oppose all measures that harm it. All the while we preserve our independence and our complete freedom of action.

The Dresden resolution does not interfere any more strongly with the independence of the French socialists than does the Kautsky resolution, for which Jaurès and his friends voted in 1900. But, as experience has shown, that resolution of 1900 was not enough, so we go one step further. One cannot hold on to tactics forever on all questions, because tactics change, as do circumstances. Liebknecht once explained this very sharply by saying that if necessary, he would change tactics twenty-four times in twenty-four hours.[19] But tactics must never contradict our basic principles. As long as we are dealing with a class state, however, the basic lines of tactics remain the same, and the proposed resolution does not ask for more.

Pablo Iglesias (Spain): The Spanish Workers Party voted for the Kautsky resolution in Paris, since we hold that socialist participation in a bourgeois government is virtually impossible, except on an exceptional basis. We will vote for the Dresden resolution and believe that its scope should be clearly defined, as it can have a big impact on all countries. The anarchists, in fact, have used the experience of the Radical Socialist cabinet [in France] against us, reproaching the fact that workers on strike in France were being massacred. Our response was that this minister [Millerand] was not our co-thinker.

It's true that there are left and right wings within every party, but we should be careful that our right does not cease being socialist! We do not want defections, but we should not forget that in reality this hesitant and mistaken attitude pushes many workers toward anarchism. We demand a clear and precise solution, so that there can be no more confusion in the minds of the working class. Socialist unity should be the result of adding homogeneous elements and not heterogeneous ones.

The Dresden resolution took on a genuinely international character. The Amsterdam Congress should ratify it. The attempt at a Vandervelde-Adler compromise should be rejected; we need a categorical and frank solution.

Léon Furnémont (Belgium): . . . The Dresden resolution aims to inflict a *capitis deminutio* [diminished capacity] on a French socialist fraction. The Vandervelde-Adler resolution specifically addressed this legitimate concern. It enshrines the same substance as the Dresden resolution, but it confines itself to setting aside all condemnation and repudiation. The Belgian section rallied to the Vandervelde-Adler resolution, mandating us to avoid any thought of ostracism. If you do not intend a condemnation, you should accept the Vandervelde-Adler resolution. They say that they don't intend to condemn, but the text and the aim of the Dresden resolution are condemnatory in character, in spite of the declarations by Bebel and Guesde. Our judgment is that condemnation should be made on specific deeds, not tendencies. The Dresden Congress, however, approved a resolution that puts tendencies on trial.

I certainly understand the concern of socialists over tactical disagreements. We are no strangers to them. I understand the concerns raised here about an international formula. But speaking of our party, where there is a majority and a minority, we have no interest in the majority excommunicating the minority. . . .

Peter Knudsen (Denmark): I stand completely on the principles of the Dresden resolution, but I cannot accept the condemnation it contains. The Paris resolution of 1900 settled the question of alliances: they are permitted, but without their dangers or corruptions. I consider the word "revisionism" to be nothing but a hollow phrase, explaining nothing.

In Denmark, socialists and radicals made an alliance to oust a ministry. This alliance was purely electoral, however; the day after the victory the radicals abandoned the socialists and the socialists fought the radical ministers.[20] It is therefore proven that electoral alliances do not negate socialist independence. We reject the absolute ban on socialist participation in government and are opposed to disowning or excluding Jaurès.

I am in favor of the Vandervelde-Adler resolution.

Karl Hjalmar Branting (Sweden): By and large I join Knudsen. We in Sweden, living under conditions of subordination and without the right to vote,[21] know how difficult it is to establish correct tactics and to follow them. It would have been best if we could have done so without alliances, but we were compelled to repeatedly support the radicals, who declared themselves in favor of universal suffrage, in order not to strengthen the conservative regime. But we always maintained our position of principle. . . .

The current struggle against clericalism in France is so important that it justifies support of the government. We have a lot of sympathy for the anticlericalism efforts of Jaurès. Those who joined the [Left] Bloc remain honest socialists.

The Dresden resolution is insulting to Jaurès. The Swedish delegates will vote for the Vandervelde-Adler motion, which reproduces the positive support of the Dresden resolution without its condemnation and ostracism. The world socialist movement is too large to be sectarian and to inflict reprimands on an individual.

Rosa Luxemburg (Poland): I did not hear anyone supporting the policy of Jaurès. Those who spoke did not wish to issue prohibitions, but nevertheless his tendency was condemned. This must be noted, and it is immense progress for international socialism.

Jaurès warns against issuing general rules that cannot be adhered to. When did Jaurès become so conscientious? He and his friends have repeatedly violated congress resolutions. The decision is a moral one, but it is immense! If we fail to do this, what is the significance of our congresses and our international solidarity?

Opportunism has turned the principle of the class struggle into a phrase. In collaboration with bourgeois parties, workers' organization turns into parliamentary propaganda; international solidarity turns into freedom of tactics. . . .

Socialist collaboration with the bourgeoisie is incompatible with the principle of the class struggle.

There is no unity possible without agreement on principles, tactics, and goal. Our divisions exist; it is a question of knowing what policy is going to be applied toward them. Vandervelde and Adler aim to erase and mitigate them; we aim to bring them into broad daylight, in accordance with the advice of Lassalle.[22]

The Dresden resolution is not perfect, it is said. There is no such thing as a perfect resolution. The Dresden resolution is nevertheless a symbol of the victory of revolutionary socialism over reformist socialism.

Jaurès: . . . I have been able to judge, in speeches by a number of orators, that there is a misunderstanding of what I believe. It's claimed, erroneously, that I opposed adoption of the Kautsky resolution in 1900, which was a question of tactics. The solution was nevertheless extremely prudent because on the one hand the Kautsky resolution, while issuing a rule, foresaw various eventualities and different hypotheses, leaving it to each national party to decide the circumstances and conditions in which the rule could change. . . .

I know well that social justice is not substantially found in the republic. I would like for there to be no misunderstanding between Bebel and me on this point. I do not turn political formalism into superstition. I don't claim that the republic by itself is a principle of progress. Nor do I fail to recognize that only the class action of the proletariat prevents the stagnation of democracy—including republican democracy. While the republic does not assure progress, there can be no economic and social progress outside of it. . . .

The proletariat is the force that always has attempted to give the unconscious movement for democracy the highest and logical form: the republic, as a symbol attached to the proletariat's hopes. That is why the republic in France historically has signified progress and freedom, which is not necessarily the same in other countries to the same degree. That is why the socialist proletariat is faithful to itself, to its deep traditions—to Babeuf, to Buonarroti, to Blanqui—when it defends the republican system and republican liberty on behalf of its class interests.

A second point in reply to Bebel on this question: you say that the republic is not immediately necessary in other countries to the same degree. But beware! The republic is the logical and highest form of democracy. If democracy is pushed back in France in its logical form—the republic—this will have a damaging impact on the other countries of Europe.

That is why it is unwise to establish, as you did yesterday, the balance of advantages and disadvantages of the bourgeois republic. The social monarchy spoken of can give the proletariat a few reforms, not out of any love for the people but out of selfishness, in order to defend the bourgeoisie against possible surprise. . . .

Jules Guesde (France): . . . For us, and for the vast majority of socialists represented at Amsterdam, socialism is at root an economic phenomenon. It emerges fully armed from capitalism, of which it is both the culmination and the corrective. To use a picturesque expression, we are the children of horsepower—meaning machines, concentration of capital, the proletarianization of work, and so on. Wherever capitalism penetrates, it gives rise to the same evils, and it sets up its millions of victims for the same struggle to the death against the same enemy. On the same class basis, there is room for unity—not only around a goal but around methods and tactics, whatever the diversity of governmental conditions. The International becomes at the same time both a possibility and a necessity, no longer in words, but in deeds and action.

Everything changes, however, when we see socialism ceasing to be an economic stage and becoming an element of the democratic movement that arose from the bourgeois revolution at the end of the eighteenth century, either its extension or its culmination. In his current way of thinking at least, Jaurès is attached to this latter conception. For that reason, logically enough, he accepts and calls for an increasingly permanent collaboration with the advanced elements of the bourgeoisie, that is to say, the democrats and republicans.

Plenary Debate

Émile Vandervelde (Belgium, reporter): . . . From the standpoint of principle, the two resolutions contain the same affirmations. The same formulations can be found in both.

The Adler-Vandervelde resolution affirms that we must first of all think of the final goal: the revolutionary transformation of capitalist society into a society of justice. It is essential to proclaim that class collaboration cannot be counterposed to the class struggle.

Does this mean that socialism should not pursue the reforms necessary to the full liberation of the proletariat? The difference between reformism and the revolutionary view is this: one supports reforms in order to ameliorate the current situation of the proletariat; the other supports reforms in order to put the proletariat in a position to install a new social system. Socialists are unanimously in favor of the second objective. [*Applause*]

The Adler-Vandervelde resolution formulates the essential principles of socialism in a positive way; the Dresden resolution presents them in a negative way. The congress should decide between the two.

The purpose of the Adler-Vandervelde resolution is to make the Dresden formula of Germany fit the national framework. It is necessary to eliminate the mark of German socialism. This is only from the point of view of form.

At bottom, the Dresden resolution seems to contain a genuine contradiction. On the one hand, it formally prohibits the participation of an isolated socialist in a bourgeois government. On the other hand, it cites the Kautsky resolution that authorizes such a thing in exceptional cases. It leaves the door both open and closed. There should be no ambiguity!

This still seems secondary to us compared to the consequences that may result from the full adoption of the Dresden resolution. It contains formulas that, if misinterpreted, could appear to be excommunications. . . .

Jean Jaurès (France): . . . I do not claim to speak on behalf of the minority that voted for the Adler-Vandervelde resolution, but only for myself and the majority of the party to which I belong.

The Dresden resolution, which was adopted by the Germans after a long theoretical and practical debate, gives rise to a multitude of ideas. I can barely touch upon these ideas and state why I am opposed to this resolution. I wish to indicate our position in the debate and our point of view within international socialism. . . .

I thoroughly acknowledge that implicitly or explicitly the Dresden resolution recognizes the dual necessity of immediate and revolutionary socialist action. It is correct in saying that socialism must be carried on by a class organization, independent in its goal and actions and devoted to the complete transformation of the capitalist system, with the objective of abolishing all exploitation and restoring to the workers collectively all the fruits of their labor.

It would appear from Vandervelde's report that to him the reformists seem to consider reforms as a means of consolidating the bourgeois regime. I know not whom he means by this, but it applies neither to me nor to my friends. All our reforms have for their revolutionary objective the emancipation of oppressed and exploited labor. [*Applause*]

We wish to be autonomous in our objective and in the political and economic organization of the working class, not isolated into factional sects but rather participating in the whole historic environment of proletarian revolutionary activity. Insofar as the Dresden resolution recognizes the necessity of socialist autonomy, I agree with it.

But you must recognize that socialism needs to make its appeal to all the forces of democracy if it is to accomplish immediate reforms. We must not cease to grasp and utilize bourgeois democracy in order to further proletarian interests whenever it is appropriate. I have heard Guesde declare, at a previous meeting where we spoke together doing socialist propaganda, that out of thirty-seven million citizens [in France], not more than two hundred thousand individuals had purely capitalist class interests. I have heard Bebel say the same thing. It would be foolish to leave this half-developed democracy to itself.

This is why it is necessary for the proletariat with its tight organization to make use of all democracy. The Radical Socialist Party of France is neither proletarian nor capitalist, counting among its members artisans of small industries and rural workers. This party will accept partial reforms such as secularization, a progressive income tax, an inheritance tax, and the progressive socialization of mines, insurance, sugar factories, and all monopolistic industries. We do not need to merge with them, but we would be fools and criminals to reject their cooperation if we might thereby realize possible reforms that would hasten the coming of the new era. [*Applause*]

What leads me to vote against the Dresden resolution is that it appears to me to be an attempt to set forth as a supreme formula of socialism what is really only a socialist tradition. To Bebel, Ferri, and Kautsky I will say that it is a singular method of establishing socialist unity in France to place a weapon in the hands of one of the factions to be used against the other.

Above all, I am opposed to the Dresden resolution because it implies a sort of deep distrust of the proletariat. Its authors seem to fear that the proletariat will compromise itself and lose itself through its collaboration with democracy. International socialism, which would renovate the entire world and free it from capitalism, tells the proletariat that it expects to accomplish this as if it were an incompetent minor incapable of directing itself—a blind man in a strange city. We oppose the Dresden resolution to protest against this position, which would limit the diverse activity of the proletariat by issuing narrow rules and binding the working class, which has the need of the greatest freedom of initiative and activity. The more mature and stronger the proletariat is in any country, the more decisively does it move toward our tactics. . . .

In seeking to force their Dresden resolution upon us, they merely communicate to the international congress the spirit of uncertainty and hesitation with which they are stricken.

You [German Social Democrats] have given to international socialism a method of action and systematic organization. You are a great party, and to you belongs the future of Germany, one of the most forceful and intelligent of the great divisions of humanity. But there is a great contrast between the appearance and the reality of your great force in spite of your electoral success. It is apparent to the eyes of all that this formidable electoral force of yours, valuable as it may be for propaganda, has little effect because you refuse to utilize democratic instruments that are necessary to give it effect.

The Dresden resolution will impose upon the whole International movement the rules of inaction and the necessity of inaction that it has imposed upon the German movement and that has taken the instruments for transformation from the German proletariat. They are lacking in revolutionary tradition. They have not conquered universal suffrage and democracy; they have received it from above, and today those who gave it threaten to withdraw it. Thus, in your "red kingdom" of Saxony you may find your universal suffrage taken away from you without the possibility of resistance.

Your publications represent me as the corrupter of the proletariat. Yet you were obliged to permit your official organ to sign a retraction at the time of the Krupp affair.[23] Why? You have no revolutionary tradition. You are the only country in the world where socialism will not be enacted when it secures a majority. You have no true parliamentary regime, for your parliament is, after all, simply a plaything in the hands of more powerful forces. You are therefore neither parliamentary nor revolutionary socialists. To be sure, you are large and strong; you have your destiny.

Humanity waited upon your congress at Dresden. *Vorwärts* proclaimed that the kingdom was yours after the election and that you would convene the International in Berlin, but the fact is that you are powerless. [*Applause*] You have blindly groped here and there, and concealed your powerlessness by taking refuge in theoretical formulas that conceal political aims. [*Applause*] And now you would seek to bind the International with all its forces, with all its powers, and make it share your temporary powerlessness, your momentary inactivity.

Where then does your movement encounter opposition? In France, Belgium, England, Switzerland—those countries where democratic life is most intense and most effective. It is just this fact that proves how your Dresden resolution is a menace to the International.

August Bebel (Germany): The speech that Comrade Jaurès has made today would give one the wholly false impression that we German Social Democrats had called forth this debate. Neither before nor since the Dresden Congress have we thought of such a thing for a moment. It is due much more to a fraction of the French comrades who believe that our Dresden resolution should be adopted as the foundation of the tactics of Social Democrats in all parliamentary-ruled countries. It is self-evident that we would decide for our own resolution, all the more so since the causes that led us to adopt it in Germany have appeared in a large number of other countries. Furthermore, events since the Paris Congress of 1900 have shown that in spite of the adoption of the Kautsky resolution, these tendencies, these practices, have continued to advance and in many countries have secured an important influence. Therefore, it is doubly desirable to pass judgment on these tendencies.

When one listened to Jaurès, the question continually arose: How is it possible that a majority could be found in the commission for such a resolution [the Dresden-Amsterdam resolution]? He has made it appear as if the other nations must be absolute idiots to vote for such a resolution. He has represented it as the abolition of all freedom, of individual thought, as a suppression of the minority, in short, as the greatest intellectual terrorism conceivable in Social Democracy. Hence, it is characteristic that a few of our friends who were not wholly in accord with all the phrases of the resolution have favored the Adler-Vandervelde one, while the entire sense and content of our resolution remains untouched. From this standpoint, Jaurès's whole critique is directed upon this resolution's content and significance. Jaurès says it belongs only to monarchical Germany.

To be sure, Germany is not just one monarchy; it is almost two dozen monarchies, and for a monarchy at the very least, two dozen too many. [*Laughter and cries of "Good!"*] So conditions in Germany are actually extraordinary. Certainly Germany is a reactionary, feudalistic, police-dominated land—one of the worst-ruled countries in Europe. We who have to fight this system day after day and who bear the traces of its workings upon our bodies know this well. We do not need anyone from other countries to tell us what miserable conditions we live in. But the facts are such that our resolution may perhaps give the correct tactics to be followed in other countries.

My opinions on monarchy and republic have been frequently given in no unmistakable manner in the bourgeois press. I repeat them now outside the commission. It goes without saying that we are republicans, socialist republicans. [*Applause*] That is indeed one of the strongest complaints against us by Count Bülow and Prince Bismarck and the whole German reaction, from all times up to the present. We have never denied this, but we do not rush after the bourgeois republic. However much we may envy you French on account of your republic, and however much we may wish it, we do not think it worthwhile to let our heads be cracked for it. [*Thunderous applause*] Whether bourgeois monarchy or bourgeois republic, both are class states. Both must, due to their very nature, be considered as supports for the capitalist social order. Both must use all their strength with the aim of having the bourgeoisie retain complete power in legislation, because the very moment that they lose political power they also lose their economic and social position.

Monarchy is not as bad as you paint it, nor is the republic as good. Even in our military, agrarian, police Germany, we have institutions that would be ideal in comparison with those of your bourgeois republic. Look at the tax legislation in Prussia and other individual states, and then look at France. I know of no other country in Europe that has such an oppressive, reactionary, and exploitative system of taxation as France. As opposed to this exhausting system with a budget of three and a half billion francs, we at least have a progressive income and property tax.

And so far as concerns the improvement of the working class, the bourgeois republic also utilizes all its forces against the workers. Where are the workers treated with more universal and oppressive brutality than in the great bourgeois republic on the other side of the ocean, the ideal of so many of you? In Switzerland too—a far more democratic republic than even France—six times this last short summer the militia was used against the workers who sought to make use of the right to organize through small strikes.

I envy you and your republic especially on account of the universal suffrage for all representative bodies. But I tell you frankly that if we had the suffrage to the same degree and with the same freedom as you, we would have shown something totally different from what you have as yet shown us. [*Tremendous applause*] When workers and employers in your country come into conflict, there arises a shriek to the high heavens against the French proletariat. What is your militia today other than a most acceptable instrument for the maintenance of class domination? There has been no great battle in the last four years—whether at Lille, Roubaix, Marseilles, Brest, Martinique, or more recently in Normandy against the striking workers—in which the Waldeck-Rousseau/Millerand ministry and the Combes ministry have not used the military against the workers.[24] In November, the Paris police broke into the Parisian labor headquarters in the most shamefully violent manner and wounded and clubbed seventy workers. At that time some of our socialist friends in the Chamber [of Deputies] refused to vote for punishing the chief of police. [*Hisses*]

Jaurès has delivered a lecture to us about what we should do. I will only tell him that if in Germany anyone had thought, for the sake of favoring the government, of supporting a measure that surrendered the most important interest of the proletariat, he would find himself on the next day without any vote. [*Tremendous applause*] He would not remain a representative of the people another hour. We are too well disciplined for that.

Jaurès said that the Dresden resolution betrayed a spirit of uncertainty and doubt. I am greatly astonished that so widely cultured and historically correct a man as Comrade Jaurès should make such a statement concerning the Dresden resolution and German Social Democracy. With the exception of Turkey and Russia, we Germans have the worst-ruled government in Europe. But in spite of that, by means of universal suffrage for the Reichstag and the corrupted suffrage in the individual states, we have sent a great number of representatives to the legislative bodies of Germany.

Have these representatives ever rejected any reform, ever refused to support any advance? Quite the contrary. If we have secured the least bit of political and social advance in Germany, we Social Democrats can ascribe it to our account alone. [*"Bravo!"*] We can do this even despite the threats of our enemy Bismarck, and despite the attacks of our friend Jaurès. [*Applause*]

Only because of us are they forced and whipped on to make reforms. The Social Democrats are so charitable as to accept all concessions that they can wring from their opponents whenever an advance is actually offered—whether today from the government, tomorrow from the Liberal parties, or the day after from the Center [Party]. But the very next hour we will fight them all—Center, government representatives, and Liberals—as our constant enemies. The bottomless abyss between us and the government, as well as the bourgeois parties, is not forgotten for a moment. . . .

If the republic of France was in danger the last few years (I accept that as a fact), you were wholly right when you worked with the bourgeois defenders of the republic to rescue it. We would have done exactly the same. Neither do we offer you any reproach for your struggle against clericalism. Unite with the Liberals for this purpose, if you alone are too weak. We would have done the same, but after the battle we go our separate ways.

And what about the threats to world peace, which Jaurès and his friends saved the world from? We too have *spoken* for world peace, but in contrast to us, you *voted* for a military and naval state [*the Jaurèsists: "No!"*], for a colonial state [*the Jaurèsists: "No!"*], for indirect taxes, for the secret fund [*objections among the Jaurèsists*], and thereby supported everything that endangered peace. [*Loud applause*] We cannot give a vote of confidence to the budget of a capitalist government.[25] [*Loud applause*]

Jaurès hopes through this cooperation with capitalist parties to secure the nationalization of railroads and mines. One of the most important points in his program, then, monarchical Germany has already accomplished. [*Laughter*] If we in Germany really wished such an advance we would naturally have also supported the bourgeois parties, but we would have rejected most decisively any permanent alliance with these elements.

Jaurès believes that for Germany, too, the Dresden resolution will have only a temporary significance. It seems to me that on this point he is a very poor prophet. I certainly can think of no conditions in which we would not act according to the resolution's fundamental principles. Therefore, I have never heard a more outrageous, contradictory assertion than that the Dresden resolution arose from a spirit of doubt and uncertainty. It was directed at just such doubters and uncertain individuals who sought to corrupt our old and tested tactics, and it is a sign of our security that we have never thought of excommunicating anybody.

Jaurès spoke further of the political powerlessness of German Social Democracy. What did he expect us to do after we had attained our three million votes? Did he expect us to set the three million in motion and lead them on toward the imperial castle? [*Laughter*] Immediately after this great victory, I said that things would not at once be very much different. Three million is not enough for us, but give us four or eight million and then we'll see. [*Loud applause*] What you expect us to do at present, when we are opposed to a capitalist majority of eight million, I certainly do not know. But just as we have never up to now taken a step backward, so in the future we shall march forward on the road of the Dresden resolution and rejoice when our opponents give way to us. [*Applause*] . . .

Victor Adler (Austria): Our amendment is the most intelligent, the simplest, and the most natural in the world, but the question itself is quite complicated.

We Austrians place ourselves absolutely on the basis of the principles contained in the Dresden resolution and the program of the Austrian party. The international congress must declare its position very clearly on our principles. The Dresden resolution may be good for Germany, but it bears a national label; it is appropriate for a specific country and a specific moment. The question currently posed is that this national resolution must be internationalized. . . .

It's not just the Jaurèsists who feel attacked by the Dresden resolution, but Social Democrats of all countries. We come here based on what unites us. We want to remove from the resolution the teeth biting our friends. [*Applause*] The Belgians and the Austrians agree that the Jaurès group's successes in France should be viewed with the greatest suspicion and with the greatest concern over the future of the proletariat. We regard these socialists as friends who are in danger of leaving the terrain they should be in. They are nevertheless our comrades of struggle, whom we tell: step back, but stay inside!

Jaurès has done the worst service to our amendment by voting for it in the commission. Our resolution in substance recognizes the Dresden resolution while disagreeing with its tactics. There were some who voted for the Dresden resolution who later tried to compromise. Bebel said that the Dresden resolution should be seen as a warning. I am all for warnings, but in my own home. International warnings are something new. It is already difficult to explain things pedagogically in one's own country. But if we do not want to issue a warning to you, Jaurès, even less do we want to give you a passport for a tactic that gives us the greatest unease, to such an extent that we believe it fatal for the proletariat in France and for its parliamentary activity. For these reasons, I regret that Jaurès voted for our amendment on behalf of his party. Perhaps this indicates that the members of his party wanted it because they themselves do not approve of the tactics of Jaurès. So it seems that his party lacks unanimity. The question therefore becomes more complex and even more difficult for us. . . .

If our amendment is rejected, we must vote for the Dresden resolution, because of the principles contained within it.

Édouard Vaillant (France): . . . There is a practical and necessary reason to reject the Adler-Vandervelde amendment and to adopt the Dresden resolution. Recalling the Kautsky resolution of 1900 demonstrates it.

We are told that the [1900] resolution unambiguously condemned the participation of a socialist in government with regard to Millerand, but at the same time possible exceptions were foreseen. We responded that this might be so, but the fact of foreseeing these and witnessing the vote in favor of it by the friends of Millerand should suffice to annul it. That is what happened.

Today the same thing is being said about the Adler-Vandervelde amendment. I know very well that what is also being condemned is revisionism, this new methodology of an alliance with the bourgeoisie, of a bloc with the capitalists. The fact that this amendment is less clear than the Dresden resolution and that it is being supported by the votes of revisionists and partisans of an alliance with the bourgeoisie suffices for it to lose the value its authors attribute to it. It is therefore important not to fall back into the error of 1900 and to vote instead for a clear antirevisionist proposal against the new methodology, which the Dresden resolution unambiguously condemns.

Doing so is all the more important since, as Adler recognized in the commission, the current compromise both in France and elsewhere is more serious than in 1900. At that time, the socialists of the new methodology had one minister in the government. Today it is they themselves who have entered into a bloc, participating in and taking responsibility for the bourgeois government. The Dresden resolution condemns such participation in France and everywhere, and affirms the need for the Socialist Party's tactics to be distinct, without any link to parties of the bourgeoisie.

By this very fact too, the Dresden resolution creates the only possible and acceptable conditions for socialist unity that we just voted for.[26] To unite with socialists in such a bloc would be to unite with a wing of the bourgeois army; it would be to join in alliance with it. Socialists should quit the bloc with the bourgeoisie and join the socialist bloc. They should unite on the only basis possible, on the expressly socialist foundation affirmed by the Dresden resolution.

For these reasons, both international and national, I and the Socialist Party of France ask you to reject the Adler-Vandervelde amendment and to vote for the Dresden resolution.

2.

The Debate on Colonialism

Introductory Note on the Colonialism Debate

During the second half of the nineteenth century, a scramble took place by a number of European countries—Britain, France, Germany, the Netherlands, Belgium, Italy, Portugal, and Spain—to build or expand colonial empires. These countries carried out in effect a division of the world, symbolized most graphically by the Berlin Conference of 1884–85, which formally carved up the African continent. By the early twentieth century, the only independent countries remaining in Africa were Liberia and Ethiopia. A similar situation of colonial and imperial rule came to prevail in major parts of Asia, the Pacific, and Latin America; toward the end of the nineteenth century, the United States and Japan joined the rush for empires.

The causes of this effort to obtain colonies and spheres of influence were fundamentally economic. During the late nineteenth century, the most developed capitalist countries of Europe and North America were increasingly dominated by industrial and trading monopolies and by a few large banks. Obtaining colonies was seen by these interests as a way to guarantee access to cheap raw materials, labor power, and fields for investment and sales. Thus was born the modern system of imperialism, which profoundly affected the international political and economic picture.

* * *

The world socialist movement had a deeply rooted tradition of solidarity with the struggles of oppressed nations. Writings by Marx and Engels on Ireland, Poland, and India, for example, were rooted in the view that "a nation cannot become free and at the same time continue to oppress other nations."[1]

That tradition was registered in two resolutions adopted by the Second International congress of 1896 that declared support for struggles by oppressed peoples. One resolution stated: "The Congress declares in favor of the full autonomy of all nationalities, and its sympathy with the workers of any country at present suffering under the yoke of military, national, or other despotisms." A second resolution called for solidarity with independence struggles in Cuba, Crete, and Macedonia. At the following congress in 1900, a resolution on colonialism was approved that condemned imperialism and colonial abuses, calling for the formation of socialist parties in the colonially dominated countries.[2]

But alongside this position, a different one began to develop. As part of his revisionist challenge to Marxism, Eduard Bernstein openly questioned the socialist movement's anticolonial stance. Writing in 1896, Bernstein proclaimed: "We will condemn and oppose certain methods of subjugating savages. But we will not condemn the idea that savages must be subjugated and made to conform to the rules of higher civilisation."[3]

At the Second International's 1904 congress in Amsterdam, delegates openly aired these counterposed views.

Hendrick van Kol, a leader of the Dutch party, presented the perspective of "socialist colonialism" to the congress—the idea that a socialist country, too, would require colonies. He and others defended the view being spread by capitalist spokespeople as to colonialism's "civilizing mission" toward the "backward natives." That perspective was also registered in a Dutch resolution submitted to the 1904 congress, reproduced in the pages below, presumably drafted by Van Kol.

As will be seen in the excerpts from the 1904 debate, there was relatively little discussion on the question at the Amsterdam Congress.

The resolution adopted in Amsterdam avoided either endorsing or opposing the procolonialist arguments. At the same, time, however, it backed off from the perspective of the 1896 resolution that gave support to at least some independence struggles. The adopted resolution instead presented an ambiguous position that limited itself to condemning colonial abuses. Its goal was "[t]o claim for the natives that liberty and autonomy, compatible with their state of development, bearing in mind that the complete emancipation of the colonies is the object to pursue." In line with such a perspective, the Amsterdam Congress then proceeded to adopt a separate resolution on India that called for "the establishment of self-government in the best form practicable by the Indians themselves (under British paramountcy)."[4]

The Amsterdam Congress of 1904 thus marked a retreat from the Second International's anticolonialist position, setting the stage for a sharp conflict at the Stuttgart Congress of 1907.

Reflecting the growth of opportunism within the Second International, the proponents of "socialist colonialism" secured an outright majority in the Stuttgart Congress's colonialism commission. Reporting for this majority to the congress plenary, Van Kol laid out its procolonialist perspective, as he had done in 1904, under the guise of adopting "positive" measures rather than simply putting forward "negative" views condemning colonial abuses.

Many readers today will undoubtedly be shocked by the openly racist views put forward by some right-wing delegates concerning indigenous peoples, whom they mocked and belittled. It should be kept in mind, however, that such views thoroughly pervaded bourgeois society at the time, expressed by leading politicians and eminent scientists alike. The pseudoscience of eugenics was then widely accepted, for example, along with other racial prejudices. Therefore, the fact that such poisonous attitudes infected even sections of the working-class and socialist movements should not be surprising.

These reactionary views, however, did not go unanswered at the congress. Opponents of colonialism vehemently rejected this antisocialist perspective and sought to establish the position of support for the worldwide struggle against colonial rule.

When the counterposed commission resolutions were brought into the congress plenary, another debate occurred. This time the full body adopted the anticolonialist perspective of the commission minority. But the traditional socialist condemnation of bourgeois colonial policy passed by a surprisingly narrow margin: 127 votes against 108, with 10 abstentions. The closeness of the vote indicated the growing strength of the opportunist trend within the Second International and its parties, foretelling what was to come.

* * *

While the procolonialist forces were pushed back at the Stuttgart Congress, the debate nevertheless highlighted one of the Second International's weak spots: the fact that it never became a truly world movement. Even though the Second International's reach extended to many countries, it was nevertheless still predominantly a European and North American movement.

One person from India did speak at the close of the debate: Bhikaiji Cama. But while Cama spoke on behalf of the oppressed people of India, she was speaking as an individual and did not represent a socialist party in her country.

More importantly, while congress resolutions gave support to various anticolonial struggles from 1896 on, those struggles remained underappreciated by most sections of the movement. Even the colonialism commission minority resolution in 1907, for example, did not call for unconditional independence for all colonies.

What was largely missing from the colonialism debates of 1904 and 1907 was a perspective of the colonial masses as agents of their own liberation. Such a view was put forward in 1913 by someone who was then a leading figure in the Second International—V. I. Lenin:[5]

> Everywhere in Asia a mighty democratic movement is growing, spreading and gaining in strength. The bourgeoisie there is *as yet* siding with the people against reaction. *Hundreds* of millions of people are awakening to life, light and freedom. What delight this world movement is arousing in the hearts of all class-conscious workers, who know that the path to collectivism lies through democracy! What sympathy for young Asia imbues all honest democrats![6]

The Colonialism Debate at the 1904 Amsterdam Congress

Proposed Resolutions

Dutch Resolution

The International Socialist Congress at Amsterdam declares that Social Democrats are obliged to define their position regarding colonial policy for the following reasons:

1. Historical development has given to several countries colonies, economically bound by close ties to their mother country, politically unaccustomed to self-government, so that it would be impossible to leave them to themselves, if only from the point of view of international relations.

2. Modern capitalism is pushing civilized countries on to continuous expansion, both to open new outlets for their products and to find fields for the easy increase of their capital. This policy of conquest—often joined with crimes and pillage, having no other aim than to quench the capitalists' insatiable thirst for gold and forcing ever greater expenditures for the increase of militarism—must be opposed implacably. It is this that leads nations along the road of protectionism and of chauvinism, constituting a perpetual menace of international conflicts and, above all, aggravating the crushing burden on the proletariat and retarding its emancipation.

3. The new wants that will make themselves felt after the victory of the working class and from the time of its economic emancipation will make necessary, even under the socialist system of the future, the

possession of colonies. Modern countries can no longer dispense with countries furnishing certain raw materials and tropical products indispensable to the industry and the needs of humanity, until such time as these can be produced by the exchange of the products of home industry and commerce.

The Social Democratic Party, which has economic development and the class struggle as the foundations of its political action, and which, in conformity with its principles, its aims, and its tendencies, severely condemns all exploitation and oppression of individuals, classes, and nations, accepts the following rules to define its colonial policy:

As capitalism is an inevitable stage of economic evolution that the colonies also must traverse, it will be necessary to make room for the development of industrial capitalism, even by sacrificing, if necessary, the old forms of property (communal or feudal).

But at the same time, the Social Democracy should struggle with all its strength against the degenerating influence of this capitalist development upon the colonial proletariat, and so much the more because it may be foreseen that the latter will not be capable of struggling for itself.

With a view to improving the condition of the laborers, as well as to prevent all the profits being taken away from the colonies, thus impoverishing them, the operation by the state of suitable industries will be useful or necessary, in conjunction with the operation of others by private parties. This will serve alike to hasten the process of capitalist development and to improve the social status of the native laborer.

It will then be the duty of the Social Democracy to favor the organization of the modern proletariat in all countries where it shall arise, to increase its strength of resistance in its struggle against capitalism, and, by raising its wages, to avert for the old capitalist countries the dangers of the murderous competition of the cheap labor of these primitive peoples.

To lift up the natives with a view to democratic self-government should be the supreme aim of our colonial policy, the details of which will be elaborated in a national program for each particular colonial group.

In view of these considerations, the Amsterdam Congress holds that it is the duty of the socialist parties of all countries:

1. To oppose by all means in their power the policy of capitalist conquest.

2. To formulate in a program the rules to be followed in their colonial policy, based on the principles enunciated in this resolution.

Plenary Debate

Hendrick van Kol (Netherlands, reporter): We had a complex problem to solve in the commission, which has not yet been fully clarified. It is to be regretted that the parties have not yet followed the Paris Congress decision to fully study the colonial question.[7]

Our views on colonial policy have thus far been purely negative, pointing with indignation to colonialism's bloody horrors. Without weakening our earlier protests or blunting its sharpness, Social Democracy is now seeking positive measures. Today we must also examine the question of what we can do both to reduce the crimes against the peoples of the colonies, on the one hand, as well as to make colonial policy less burdensome and harmful for the proletariat of the colonizing countries.

The colonies exist. What should be done with them? The tendency toward colonization is general and has persisted throughout history.

Perhaps the day will come when Europe will have to make do without colonies. If [Joseph] Chamberlain's plan succeeds, and if the British Empire builds a customs system containing one-fourth of the earth's surface and one-seventh of its population, then we will no longer see a market for our products.[8] A crisis will erupt and unemployment will rise, perhaps resulting in the social revolution. The colonial question will then become more important than the social question itself.

We must obviously protest against the violent expansion of colonialism, as we are enemies of all conquest even if we don't necessarily consider colonial property to be a blessing for the colonizing country. Colonialism today enriches a few large trading houses and shipping companies, while the burden is borne by the proletariat of the colonizing countries.

Unfortunately, it is now very difficult to propose positive measures, because the colonized countries are at very different levels of economic development, and there are different races of people. Should one seek to preserve the indigenous forms of social life? Can we prevent the advance of capitalism? I'm just asking the questions.

We are representatives of historical evolution and progress, and we defend law and justice. We fight to free the native population from boundless misery and savagery, while protecting it from the sufferings of capitalism.

The focus of all colonial reform is, of course, self-government. We cannot yet say exactly what the positive measures are, but for the first time Social Democracy has formulated positive demands in the right direction.

May the proletariat be worthy of its great cause, given the importance that the colonial question has for the development of all humanity. A socialist state will also have colonies, but the socialist party will prevent the exploitation and torture of indigenous peoples and will protest against the hypocritical actions of different religions.

Modeste Terwagne (Belgium): The commission's solution was a compromise, because within the commission we were far from agreement. As for me, I support the ideas put forward by Van Kol on colonial reform. Socialist parties should set up commissions responsible for studying the colonial question and for developing socialist propaganda in the colonies.

Jules Uhry (France, French Workers Party): I accept the commission's resolution, but I have some reservations about Van Kol's comments about peaceful colonial expansion. History proves that colonial expansion cannot be peaceful.

Adopted Resolution

That this Congress, considering the ever more costly capitalist exploitation of an ever-extended colonial territory—exploitation not regulated and not restrained, which wastes capitals and natural riches, exposes the colonial populations to the most cruel, most terrible, and often the bloodiest oppression, and serves only to aggravate the misery of the proletariat;

Mindful of the resolution of the Paris Congress (1900) on the colonial question and imperialist policy;

Declares that it is the duty of the national socialist parties and of the parliamentary groups:

1. To oppose without any compromise every imperialist or protectionist measure, every colonial expedition, and all military expenses for the colonies.

2. To fight every monopoly, every concession of vast territories, to prevent the wealth of the colonial territory from being appropriated by the all-powerful capitalists.

3. To denounce incessantly the deeds of oppression of which the natives are the victims, to obtain for them the most efficacious measures of protection against military acts of cruelty or capitalist exploitation, to prevent them from being robbed of their possessions, either by violence or by deceit.

4. To propose or to favor all that is conducive to the amelioration of the natives' conditions of life, public works, hygienic measures, schools, etc.; to do their utmost to withdraw them from the influence of the missionaries.

5. To claim for the natives that liberty and autonomy, compatible with their state of development, bearing in mind that the complete emancipation of the colonies is the object to pursue.

6. To try to bring the control of international policy—which, as the natural consequence of the capitalist system, is more and more influenced by financial gangs—under parliamentary control.

The Colonialism Debate at the 1907 Stuttgart Congress

Proposed Resolutions

Commission Minority Resolution (Adopted by Plenary)

The Congress is of the opinion that capitalist colonial policy, by its very nature, must lead to enslavement and compulsory labor or to the extermination of the native population of the colonial territories.

The civilizing mission, to which capitalist society appeals, serves only as a cover for a burning passion for conquest and exploitation. Only with the achievement of the socialist society will it be possible for all peoples to develop themselves to a complete civilization.

Capitalist colonial policy, instead of increasing the productive forces, by the very fact that it enslaves and pauperizes the natives, as well as the damage that it inflicts by war, destroys the natural riches of the countries in which it plants its methods. It renders slower or hinders thereby the very development of commerce and of the sale of the industrial products of the civilized states.

The Congress condemns the barbaric methods of capitalist colonization and demands in the interest of the development of the productive forces a policy that guarantees the peaceful development of civilization and places the natural riches at the disposal of the entirety of humanity.

In reaffirmation of the Paris (1900) and Amsterdam (1904) resolutions, the Congress repudiates colonization, as at present carried on, since being of a capitalist character, it has no other aim but to conquer new countries and to subjugate their populations in order to exploit them mercilessly for the benefit of an insignificant minority, while increasing the burden on the proletariat at home.

The Congress, as an enemy of all exploitation of man by man, and the defender of all oppressed without distinction of race, condemns this policy of robbery and conquest, this shameless application of the right of the strong trampling underfoot the rights of the vanquished races; and further states that this colonial system increases the danger of international complications and war, thus making heavier the financial burdens for navy and army.

From the financial point of view, the colonial expenses—both those that arise from imperialism and those that are necessary to further the economic evolution of the colonies—must be borne by those who profit from the spoliation of the colonies and derive their wealth therefrom.

The Congress declares finally that it is the duty of the socialist members of parliament to oppose without compromise in their respective parliaments the regime of exploitation and serfdom that prevails in all colonies of today, to exact reforms for the amelioration of the condition of the natives, to safeguard their rights by preventing their exploitation and enslavement, and to work with every means at their disposal for the education of these races to independence.

Commission Majority Resolution

The Congress, while pointing out that in general the usefulness or necessity of colonies, especially in the working class, is greatly exaggerated, does not condemn in principle and for all time every colonial policy, which under a socialist regime may become a work of civilization.

In reaffirmation of the Paris (1900) and Amsterdam (1904) resolutions . . . [*The next four paragraphs are exactly the same as those from the commission minority resolution above.*]

To this effect, the socialist members of parliament must propose to their governments to create an international understanding with a view to establish an international agreement for the protection of the right of the aborigines, the execution of which shall be mutually guaranteed by the contracting countries.

Commission Debate

Eduard David (Germany): Previous congresses have already taken up the colonial question and voted on resolutions. But readopting these resolutions is not enough. Our task here is to give clear direction for the practical activity of Social Democracy. We must condemn the type of colonization carried out by the bourgeois world today. At the same time, we must use all our influence to protect the colonies' population and their natural resources from the exploitation of the capitalists. We should do so in the same way that we struggle for laws to protect workers in the civilized countries in the fight against capitalism.

Bebel expressed this thought in the German Reichstag:

> It is not necessarily a crime, in itself, to engage in colonial policy. Under certain circumstances, colonial policy can be a work of civilization. It is a question of knowing how colonial policy is to be carried out. There is a big difference between what colonial policy should be and what it is. If the representatives of the nations of culture and civilization, such as those of Europe and North America, go to foreign peoples as liberators, as friends and civilizers, in order to bring the benefits of culture and civilization, to raise them to the level of modern people—if all this is done with a noble intention and in a just way, then we Social Democrats will be the first to support such colonization as a civilizing mission.

I therefore ask that we adopt a resolution stating that the socialist congress accepts colonization in principle, on the grounds that occupying and making use of the entire world is indispensable for the well-being of humanity. At the same time, however, it is understood too that the resolution must also criticize the work of capitalism today.

Europe needs colonies. It does not have enough of them. Without colonies, we would be comparable from an economic point of view to China.

Georg Ledebour (Germany): I cannot accept David's opinion, and in a certain sense I must also speak against Bebel. Comrade David has missed the main point. As long as we have a capitalist world, colonial policy will always display the same abominable characteristics that we condemn. David appears to believe that these atrocities are avoidable and are characteristic only of present-day colonial policies. That is a fundamental error.

David read a supposed statement by Bebel to back up his point of view. It does not come from an authoritative statement by Bebel, but from a remark made in passing during one of his many Reichstag speeches on colonial questions. As I understand Bebel's position, he would vigorously protest David's interpretation of his words. Simply picking sentences out of context is unacceptable. In itself, these sentences certainly oblige me to polemicize against Bebel too. They can be interpreted to mean that the existing horrors of colonialism can be avoided in today's capitalist states. But present-day colonialism is the inevitable result of capitalism. Only through the resistance of the exploited themselves can these brutalities be lessened, but the colonial peoples cannot accomplish this, because their capacity to resist is virtually nonexistent.

In our resolution we must emphasize that we do not expect capitalist colonization to exercise any civilizing mission. As a matter of principle we are opposed to all exploitation and oppression in our own countries, and we must fight equally against the much greater exploitation and oppression in the colonies. With this declaration of principle at its head, our resolution then can further explain that as a minority of German society, we are for the greatest possible protection of the native peoples through the creation of colonial laws protecting their rights. We all agree on this. But here is the main thing: nobody must get the idea from our resolution that we think capitalist colonial policy is capable of freeing itself from the abominations that characterize it.

Modeste Terwagne (Belgium): I speak on behalf of the minority of my party. For us Belgians the question is: Should we leave the Congo in its current state, or do we want to better conditions there? . . .

Do not close the door to the future! If from one day to the next colonial production were ended, industry would be seriously damaged. It logically follows that men utilize all the riches of the globe, wherever they may be situated. . . .

I therefore recommend the amendment that I introduced and that moreover was in the original draft of the text proposed by Van Kol: "The congress therefore does not reject in principle every colonial policy. Under a socialist regime, colonization could be a force for civilization."

Gustave Rouanet (France): I believe it is wrong to consider colonization as a purely capitalist phenomenon. Colonization is also a historical fact. For this reason, I support Terwagne's resolution [amendment]. It is possible today to obtain considerable improvements in the colonies. The colonial question is an international question, and the rights of the natives must also be established internationally.

The European and American civilized peoples find themselves with enormous spaces. Should they not use these spaces to better the economic existence of their countries? I say yes. So the question of colonization must be examined, even bourgeois colonization. The question of colonization should be considered as an international question and not a national one, because colonies are increasingly becoming international.

We must reduce to a minimum the advantages that the bourgeoisie monopolizes in the colonies, and I ask that the rights of the natives be increased.

Colonial laws must be established. I urge you to employ all your energy not to fight colonization—which is in fact impossible to prevent—but to mitigate the lot of the natives and to give them the same rights as whites.

Engelbert Pernerstorfer (Austria): I cannot agree with Ledebour's ideas of rigid negativity. He claims that colonial policy is a consequence of capitalism and that we must therefore fight and protest against it.

We don't say: "Let's wait for socialism to improve the economic situation." So we should not say, "Let's wait for socialism to deal with the colonies." We are trying to improve the conditions of the proletariat. As for the colonies: they exist. We must participate in colonial policy and transform it in the direction of our ideas. We are for positive collaboration.

I agree with Terwagne's ideas, and I accept the introductory wording proposed by David.

A. H. Lawrence (Britain): I recognize that the capitalist colonial system is barbaric and is far from favoring the development of civilization. But the current discussion should be based on practice. If we don't concern ourselves with the colonies, the capitalists will utilize the native peoples against the European proletariat and make them forces of reaction.

Emmanuel Wurm (Germany): The main question in the discussion has been neglected. In my view the question is posed as follows: Based on working-class interests, what will be our attitude with regard to the colonial policy followed by the capitalists?

Colonial policy does not depend on our will or desire, but is carried out without us and against us. Colonial policy burdens us with growing budgets and also increases the danger of war. It's from this point of view that the resolution must be considered.

Pernerstorfer says: " We should not have a negative policy." We agree. But the search for means to eliminate the abuses and cruelties is an eminently positive policy. We cannot take responsibility for colonial policy but must reject it and protest against it. Such protest is not an empty phrase. It is educational; it is propaganda; it is deeply socialist. We cannot follow an opportunist policy in order to be in good graces with governments and to be considered by them as having equal rights with bourgeois parties. We have nothing in common with the capitalist rulers. We can only follow a policy of principle, and that is why we must reject all colonial policy.

I propose we reject the amendment by David and Van Kol, and add to the resolution the following text: "Colonial policy increases the danger of war and the contradictions among the colonial countries, and it increases the burden on the people to support armies and navies."

Karski (Julian Marchlewski, Poland): Terwagne's reasoning is based on a fundamental error. Colonial policy and the capitalist economy are two completely different things. We can modify capitalist organization, but we cannot change colonial policy, which is based on the subjugation of one people by another. We can therefore only protest against colonial policy, because if we accept it, we take responsibility for its inevitable consequences.

Plenary Debate

Hendrick van Kol (Netherlands, reporter): We are not here to listen to fine speeches and make fine declarations, but to adopt resolutions involving the tactics of international Social Democracy. I will therefore not speak to you about questions we all agree on. We all condemn the mistreatment that the natives are victims of. We all fight capitalist colonialism. I limit myself to explaining that there were two opposing tendencies in the commission. One was negative and the other positive; one theoretical and the other practical and action oriented.

Our duty is to pursue a policy of action. Before 1870 we were a small group and still believed in the theory of capitalist collapse. Back then we thought it enough to simply protest against capitalism, point out to our followers their dreadful sufferings, and explain the sharp contrast between the reality they knew and the paradise of the future. Now we recognize that we must also carry out actions against capitalism. We must have a program of reform, and that applies to colonial policy as well.

A large majority of the commission adopted a resolution that, in my opinion, abandons the purely negative point of view and calls for a socialist colonial policy. The minority resolution, on the contrary, reveals a spirit of desperation and doubt. I don't understand how a Social Democrat who knows our theories can sign such a resolution. Ledebour will surely agree that in Europe capitalism was unavoidable—a necessary and inevitable stage of development. Should not the same also be true about capitalism in the colonies? . . .

Certainly the crimes of colonialism are abominable. But it is not true that we are unable to reduce them and mitigate colonial policy. We Dutch are one of the oldest colonizing peoples. But we have reached the point where murder, torture, burning, and plundering are no longer everyday occurrences in the Dutch colonies.

Ledebour's plans are completely utopian. He cannot be certain that a future colonial policy based on humane principles will always be entirely limited to peaceful means. I would very much regret if such a great nation as Germany were to indulge in utopian plans and limit itself at present to pure negativity. The question of the colonies is a great problem that will dominate modern history. It is therefore necessary to establish a socialist colonial policy.

The minority resolution also denies that the productive forces of the colonies can be developed through capitalist colonial policy. I do not understand at all how a thinking person can say that. Simply consider the colonization of the United States of North America. Without it the native peoples there would today still be living in the most backward social conditions.

Does Ledebour want to take away the raw materials that the colonies produce, indispensable for modern society? Does he want to renounce the vast resources of the colonies, even if only for the present? Do those German, French, and Polish delegates who signed the minority resolution want to accept responsibility for simply abolishing the present colonial system?

As long as humanity has existed there have been colonies, and I think that they will exist for centuries to come. Surely there are few socialists who think that colonies will be unnecessary in the future social order, although we do not need to discuss this question today. I ask Ledebour: Does he have the courage now, under capitalism, to renounce colonies?

Perhaps Ledebour can also tell us what he would do about the overpopulation of Europe. Where would the people who must emigrate go, if not to the colonies? What does Ledebour want to do with the growing production of European industry if he does not want to create new export markets in the colonies? And does he as a Social Democrat want to shirk his duty to work continually for the education and cultural advancement of the backward peoples? . . .

Especially for Germany's sake, I regret that Social Democrats there have limited themselves to questioning the need for colonies and the benefits they bring. You saw in the last election campaign how the masses were hypnotized by the thought of the benefits to be gained from the colonies—not only the petty bourgeoisie but also the industrial workers.[9] . . .

The task of the congress is to see to it that hope of a better future is offered to the millions of unfortunate peoples in the colonies through the practical work of the Social Democracy. [*Applause from British and Dutch delegates*]

Harry Quelch (Britain): The Social Democratic Federation that I represent here defends the minority resolution. What we criticize in the majority resolution is the first line, which does not constitute a rejection in principle of colonial policy, but limits itself to noting that the usefulness of the colonies has been exaggerated.

In our view colonial policy is criminal by its very essence. I also oppose calling for an international colonial code, since it would be absurd to demand that the exploiters protect the proletariat that they exploit. How can we have confidence in diplomatic meetings and conferences at The Hague, which in reality are nothing but "thieves' suppers," as we call them in English.[10] . . .

Eduard Bernstein (Germany): I support the majority resolution which, contrary to what the preceding speaker said, does not at all justify capitalist colonial policy. We are all opponents of such exploitation. Where we differ is how to express that opposition, the manner in which to oppose it.

As the power of socialism grows in a number of countries, so too does our responsibility. For that reason we cannot maintain a purely negative point of view on colonial matters. As Van Kol said, we must pursue a positive socialist policy. [*"Bravo!"*]

We must reject the utopian notion of abandoning the colonies. The logical consequence of such a view would be to give the United States back to the Indians. [*Commotion*] The colonies are there; we must come to terms with that. Socialists too should acknowledge the need for civilized peoples to act somewhat like guardians of the uncivilized.

Lassalle and Marx both recognized this. In the third volume of *Capital,* Marx wrote: "The earth does not belong to one people, but to all of humanity. Every people must administer it for the good of humanity."[11] And Lassalle once said, "The right of a people to its own development is as little an absolute right as any you will find. It is tied to the condition that there be some development. But people who do not develop may justifiably be subjugated by peoples who have achieved civilization."

To a large degree our economies are based on the extraction from the colonies of products that the native peoples have no idea how to use. . . .

Georg Ledebour (Germany): I am here defending the resolution of the minority. Above all we oppose the first sentence of the majority resolution, where it primarily asserts the usefulness of colonies for the workers.

However, the same Van Kol—who is the father of this resolution—demonstrated in his report that Holland's colonial policy is firstly a misfortune for the natives and secondly a misfortune for the [Dutch] workers. [*"Very good!"*] This is what Van Kol must have seen from his personal experience in the Dutch colonies.[12] But despite this, he presents us with a resolution that does not touch on these ideas. And he reproaches *us* with inconsistency! . . .

I now come to Bernstein. If we followed his method of colonial policy, we would get lost in the capitalist swamp. I remind you that Bernstein, together with a few Fabians and English socialists, made the error of siding with the British Jingoes in the Boer War. At that time he was even more imperialist than the English Liberals. He was a supporter of incorporating the Transvaal into Great Britain.[13] . . .

Unlike Bernstein, I reject the tutelage of one people over another. I ask the congress to reject such principles of subjugation.

Eduard David (Germany): . . . Ledebour thinks that colonial policy cannot be reformed, and he then declares that socialists must defend reforms to mitigate the situation of the natives. When someone shows himself to be so illogical, he has no right to accuse others of illogicality.

The [commission] minority says that it is not possible to mitigate colonial policy, that it invariably harms both the native peoples and the colonizing country. Then to be consistent the minority must advocate that the colonies be abolished. [*"Very true!"*]

Ledebour: That is what we want! [*Enthusiastic shouts of "Indeed!"*]

David (continues): If the partisans of the Ledebour resolution were actually in a position to abandon the colonies, it would mean giving them back to the native peoples. What then would happen in the colonies? It would then not be humane sentiments that triumph but barbarism. [*"Very true!"*] . . .

The colonies, as well, must go through a stage of capitalist development. You cannot simply leap from barbarism to socialism. [*"Very good!"*] Nowhere is humanity spared the painful passage through capitalism. The scientific outlook of Karl Marx makes very clear that this stage is a precondition for the socialist organization of society.

Karski (Julian Marchlewski, Poland): We must reject the last paragraph of the majority resolution, because it is illogical. We can no more speak of a "socialist colonial policy" than of a "socialist state."

David has asserted the right of one nation to exercise tutelage over another nation. But we Poles know the real meaning of this tutelage, since both the Russian tsar and the Prussian government have exercised tutelage over us. [*"Very good!"*] . . .

David quotes Marx to support his view that every nation must go through capitalism. But he is wrong to do so here. What Marx said was that countries that had already begun capitalist development would have to continue the process through to completion. But he never said that this was an absolute precondition for all nations.[14]

David also asserts that we can no longer oppose colonial policy in principle since we are supporters of colonial reforms. I answer him that we are against militarism in principle, and nevertheless we support military reforms that lighten the burden on the proletariat, such as the reduction of service time.

We socialists understand that there are other civilizations besides those of capitalist Europe. We have absolutely no right to be conceited about our so-called civilization, nor to impose it on the Asiatic peoples with their ancient civilizations that are perhaps even more advanced. [*"Bravo!"*] David thinks that the colonies would sink back into barbarism if left to themselves. In India's case that hardly seems likely. Rather, I picture that if independent, India would continue to profit from the influence of European civilization in its future development, and it would grow in this way to its fullest potential. I therefore ask you to vote for the minority resolution.

Ramsay MacDonald (Britain): I speak in the name of the Labour Party of Great Britain, and I regret that none of the resolutions note the special situation of our country. Most British colonies are inhabited by British people, who have established free states that possess complete autonomy, with some having their own parliaments. The resolutions submitted to us relate exclusively to the domains of the Crown. So I think they need more precision, especially the resolution of the majority.

I too believe we must have the courage to face the situation, and to draft a program related to colonial policy. One cannot always indulge in negativity. Such a policy rejects the masses in a type of backhanded imperialism. In making use of the colonies, questions of administration are the most important, above all when administrations depend on special bodies and not parliaments. I therefore think that international treaties offer us better results than national ones, which only serve national interests. In the realm of colonial policy, the capitalists cannot do whatever they want, as they are subject to parliamentary control.

Next Wednesday, the British government will hear from me very severe words on the abuses perpetrated in the colonies. This shows you that we are fulfilling our duty. I therefore ask you to accept the majority's resolution in the interests of our practical work. [*"Very good!"*]

Alexandre Bracke (France): I am a supporter of the minority resolution. Van Kol reproaches us for indulging in negativity. The opposite is true. The minority accepts all the positive recommendations of the majority. But the majority's resolution lacks precision, in that it does not absolutely condemn capitalist colonial policy. We know only of colonial policy practiced by capitalism, and this is what we must fight. The majority forgets to tell us the character of the colonial policy it thinks should be followed. I believe it is completely utopian to expect capitalist governments to pursue a humane colonial policy. . . .

Karl Kautsky (Germany): I was not present at the deliberations of the German delegation at which the new wording of the first paragraph was discussed, and I just read it now. Unfortunately, I see myself compelled to fight the amendment, just as I will fight the original text. [*"Bravo!"*]

How is it that the notion of a "socialist colonial policy" has found so many followers in our ranks here, when it appears to me to be a logical contradiction? Until now we have never heard anything about a "socialist colonial policy." I attribute its popularity to the newness of the idea, which has suddenly sprung up overnight. Further, it is linked to other ideas that are quite correct and necessary but are connected only superficially with colonial policy and in reality have absolutely nothing to do with it. Among these are two ideas that cannot be rejected out of hand. First is the idea that we cannot simply ignore the colonies. We have certain tasks to carry out there, and we must act as much as possible in a positive manner. As far as I know, nobody has disputed this.

Our tasks in the colonies are fundamentally the same as those at home. They are to protect the people against capitalist exploitation and against the oppression of bureaucracy and militarism—in other words, to advance social and democratic policies. That, however, is something quite different from colonialism. Colonial policy signifies the violent conquest and seizure by force of an overseas land. I contest the notion that democracy and social policy have anything to do with conquest and foreign rule. [*"Bravo!"*]

It was further said that we have a civilizing role to play and so must go out to these backward peoples as teachers and counselors. I completely agree with what Bebel said in the Reichstag. We ourselves have an interest in seeing that these primitive peoples attain a higher culture. But I disagree that colonial policy, the conquest and seizure of foreign lands, is necessary for that. Indeed I maintain that colonial policy is fundamentally detrimental to the ability to play a civilizing role. [*"Very true!"*]

A widespread misconception exists that backward peoples are hostile to the civilization brought them by more advanced peoples. On the contrary, all of our experience shows that when we approach the savages in a friendly manner, they willingly accept the tools and aid of the higher civilization. But if we come to oppress and enslave them, if they are to be brought under the tutelage of some despotism, no matter how benevolent, they will be mistrustful. Then they will reject the foreign civilization along with the foreign domination. Then it will come to wars and devastation. Everywhere we see this colonial policy practiced, it produces rebellion and degradation of the people. Even a socialist regime could not change this at all. It would likewise be obliged to view the colonies as alien bodies and establish domination over them. If we want to have a civilizing effect on the primitive peoples, then it is first necessary to win their confidence. And we will win it only by giving them their freedom. [*"Bravo!"*]

Bernstein wants to convince us that the policy of conquest is a law of nature. I am quite astonished that he defended here the theory that there are two groups of peoples, one destined to rule and the other destined to be ruled; that there are peoples who, like children, are incapable of governing themselves. That is only a variation on the old refrain, the postulate of all despotism, that some people are born into this world to be riders, with spurs on their feet, and others with saddles on their backs to carry them. This is the same argument of the slave masters in South America, who claimed that civilization was based on forced slave labor and that countries would return to barbarism if slavery was abolished. We must not accept this argument.

Bernstein's reference to Marx is incorrect. Marx certainly said that the earth belongs to the human race. But it is not the human race that is carrying out a colonial policy today. [*"Very good!"*] Marx did not say that the earth belongs to the capitalist nations. [*"Very good!" Speaking time has run out.*]

In conclusion, I ask you not to accept the introductory paragraph. It is quite new, has not been given sufficient consideration, and contradicts our whole socialist and democratic way of thinking. [*"Very true!"*] You must at least give us time to discuss it thoroughly and give it adequate consideration. We cannot accept this completely new idea of a "socialist colonial policy."

Algie Martin Simons (United States): The colonial question is very important for us Americans, as we are at the beginning of a new American colonial policy. America has sent a whole army of teachers to the Philippines, but it has also sent plenty of soldiers and cannons. In the name of civilization, they have spilled rivers of blood.[15] [*"Very true!"*] The capitalist state and the capitalist system exist for profit, and with that motive they exploit indigenous and foreign labor. For that reason, American colonial policy is also a consequence of capitalist rule.

In my opinion, a socialist colonial policy is inconceivable. The socialist society of tomorrow, which will not be based on profit and will not rest on exploitation of foreign races, will not have a colonial policy. It cannot and will have no need to do so. We conceive of the socialist system as a fraternal union of nations and races, and not a system in which one is above the other and treats the other as inferior. . . .

Gustave Rouanet (France): I regret that I don't have time to respond to the attacks of Kautsky, Ledebour, and Bracke, but I would like our adversaries to explain one thing. They tell us there is no such thing as a socialist colonial policy and that Social Democracy can only protest against colonial policy in theory and in principle. But then I ask by what strange mental aberration, after stigmatizing the barbarous methods of capitalist colonial policy, your resolution states the following: "The Congress condemns the barbaric methods of capitalist colonization and demands, in the interest of the development of the productive forces, a policy that guarantees the peaceful development of civilization and places the natural riches at the disposal of the entirety of humanity."

Please tell me whom you are addressing this demand to. You are demanding this of bourgeois society, and you are demanding that present-day society, in place of its brutalities, adopt a socialist colonial policy—something you declare to be impossible! Or do you want to develop the productivity of these countries, putting their resources at the service of a higher evolution of humanity, without occupying the colonies? You are therefore compelled to take possession of these lands, and in reality you are proclaiming the principle of a colonial policy, but without saying so. Don't you also say that very often capitalist colonial policy, by annihilating the treasures of civilization instead of developing them, pursues a goal contrary to the one that should be pursued?

In light of these contradictions, I urge you to adopt the majority resolution. . . .

Van Kol: I had not planned to speak again. But now that Kautsky has thrown the entire weight of his knowledge and international reputation into the scales, I must try to refute his arguments.

Various comrades have said that there is no way to improve the economies of the colonies. That is false and contradicts the history of colonial policy. Through our socialist activity in the Dutch parliament we have achieved significant advantages for our colonies. Why should we help only the workers of Europe and not those of other parts of the earth? Arrayed against us in Europe are mighty forces of capitalism. Why should we not also take up the struggle against capitalism in other continents? Nowhere else could we achieve easier and bigger victories than there.

Ledebour said the majority's efforts are reactionary. I simply do not understand how he, as a man of science, can fail to recognize that the colonies must first pass through a stage of capitalist development before you can begin to think of socialism there. We are working for the revolutionary development of the colonies in order to facilitate the transformation of the feudal state into a modern one, through capitalism to socialism. A leap from barbarism to socialism is impossible. [*"Very true!"*] To deny this is not only unscientific but stupid and shortsighted. Why in God's name should we not be able to raise constructive demands for this development, just as we do for the questions of militarism and the tax laws?

The American socialist movement is still young, but it would be painful to me if they refused to intervene in colonial policy and left it to [Theodore] Roosevelt's initiative. I ask the comrades of America to intervene in colonial policy, precisely in the interest of the unfortunate inhabitants of the Philippines, victims of social misery, unable to resist the invasion. [*"Bravo!"*] We have heard even today the old story about colonial crimes, which in socialist parliaments becomes boring in the long run!

I have a lot of respect for Kautsky as a man and as a fighter, but I would never have dared assume that he would allow himself to develop such unscientific theories as he has done here today. Kautsky maintains the thesis that "colonial policy is conquest, is imperialism." This formula is completely wrong. You should learn better grammar! Today, to be sure, colonial policy is imperialist. But it *does not have to be.* It can be democratic as well. In any case it is a grave error of Kautsky's to put colonial policy conceptually on a par with imperialism. I hope he will see that this is unjustified, and will strive to make good the error.

Kautsky said that we must win the confidence of the native peoples. How does he hope to win the confidence of millions of people of other skin colors if he does nothing for them? [*"Very good!"*] We in Holland have the duty and the right to tell the comrades of other countries about our experiences. We Dutch socialists have gained the confidence of millions of Javanese. But in Africa the people know nothing about the

German Social Democracy because until now it has not done its duty. If you want to win the confidence of the native peoples, then you must actively engage yourselves in the colonial question.

Our friend Kautsky made matters even worse with his advice on how to develop the colonies industrially. We are supposed to take the machines and tools to Africa! A theoretical pipe dream! That's supposed to civilize the country!

Suppose we bring a machine to the Negroes of Central Africa. What will they do with it? Perhaps they will start up a war dance around it. [*Loud laughter*] Or increase by one the number of their innumerable gods. [*Laughter*] Perhaps we should send some Europeans to run the machines. What the native peoples would do with them, I do not know. But perhaps Kautsky and I should make the attempt and accompany the machines to the Black Continent. Perhaps theory and practice would then go hand in hand into that savage land with the tools and machines. Perhaps the natives will destroy our machines. Perhaps they will kill us, or even eat us, and then I fear that given my superior corporeal development [*rubs his belly*] I would have precedence over Kautsky. [*Laughter*] If we Europeans go there to Africa with tools and machines, we would be defenseless victims of the natives. Therefore we must go there with weapons in hand, even if Kautsky calls that imperialism. [*"Very true!" from part of the hall*]

Furthermore, the natives suffer now under the tyrannical rule of individual princes. They are nearly defenseless against these princes and are exploited in the most inhumane manner. I am dubious whether a fighting proletariat will arise there under such conditions. The natives are not aware of any needs. They run around naked, without clothes, and nourish themselves from what nature offers them. Consequently they have capitalism in its most dreadful form and no proletariat that can resist it. No, in such conditions, where no law offers protection either for the natives or for immigrants, it is impossible to develop the economy in Kautsky's fashion.

Comrades, the time for words must end. We must work in a practical way for the masses of the poor and destitute in our colonies. I therefore hope that you will adopt the majority resolution by a large majority. [*Applause from several benches*]

Bhikaiji Cama (India): I bring the socialists assembled here the fraternal greetings of countless thousands of Indians, who suffer under the brutal yoke of British despotism. India pays a heavy price for British capitalist rule. Much has been said here about economic questions. What then is the economic situation of India? Each year India must pay £35 million to Britain, and not a penny of it finds its way back to India. This economic relationship causes the periodic famines and desperate poverty of countless people, innumerable epidemics, and a mortality rate that has risen to an unspeakable level.

I address here the tribunal of human justice. What is socialism if not justice? And if there is justice, why must millions of unfortunate Indians endure such agony? [*Loud applause*] India is a possession of the British Crown, a subjugated country ruled by despotism and unbearable tyranny, inhabited by a fifth of the world's population.

I call on the congress to raise its protest against this vicious tyranny. [*Applause*] . . .

Indians demand their human rights, their autonomy, their striving for independence and justice. They want the right to self-determination. Their cause is a just one. [*Loud applause*]

3.

The Debate on Immigration

Introductory Note on the Immigration Debate

In the late nineteenth and early twentieth centuries, immigration became a world political issue of increasing importance. In the United States over twenty million immigrants arrived between 1880 and 1920. In Argentina the figure was close to five million. In Australia it was around a million.

Most of these immigrants came from Europe, but not all of them. The arrival of nonwhite immigrants from Asia and Africa gave rise to significant racist campaigns in the United States and Australia in particular. In 1882, the US Congress adopted the Chinese Exclusion Act, barring immigration from China and making it nearly impossible for those who had already come to obtain citizenship. This law was renewed by Congress in 1892 and made indefinite in 1904. The state of California enacted laws excluding Japanese immigrants as well.

Australia adopted an even more restrictive approach. The Immigration Restriction Act of 1901 established a "White Australia" policy that effectively halted the entry of non-European immigrants into the country.

The racist laws in the United States and Australia found support among major sections of the organized labor movements of these countries. In 1902, the American Federation of Labor issued a pamphlet, *Some Reasons for Chinese Exclusion*, filled with racist stereotypes and assertions about Asian immigrants. For their part, Australian unions were among the biggest supporters of the White Australia policy.

Some socialists also succumbed to the pressure, promoting hostility and racism toward immigrants. Right-wing US socialist Victor Berger, for example, stated that the country would soon have five million "yellow men" "invading" each year. If something were not done, he warned, "this country is absolutely sure to become a black-and-yellow country within a few generations," adding that "Negroes and mulattoes constitute a lower race."[1]

* * *

During the 1890s, the Second International began to address the immigration issue. In 1893 a resolution urged trade unions and socialist parties to champion arriving immigrants, calling for the workers' movement "to extend among the latter the organization and the propagation of the principles of international solidarity."

At the 1896 congress, a motion put forward by Edward Aveling on behalf of a number of British labor organizations stated that trade unions "should not appeal for restrictive legislation against the immigration of aliens." That motion was adopted. A second resolution adopted in 1896 called for solidarity with Italian immigrant workers in Switzerland who had been targeted by anti-immigrant rioting that forced thousands from their homes.[2]

Nevertheless, the influence of anti-immigrant sentiment within the socialist movement was increasingly felt.

In 1903, the immigration question came up at a meeting of the International Socialist Bureau, made up of representatives of the main Second International parties. Émile Vandervelde from Belgium raised the matter of proposals in France to limit immigration of Belgian workers. In the discussion, several of those present proceeded to speak of immigration from Africa and Asia. Henry Hyndman from Britain mentioned how "the introduction of Asian labor in Europe and America raises an extremely serious economic question," while Richard Fischer from Germany spoke of how "introducing Negro or Chinese labor" into a country threatened "workers of a higher culture." Other speakers, however, opposed this perspective. The meeting eventually adopted a resolution opposing restrictions on Belgian immigration to France, while deciding to add an immigration point to the agenda of the Second International's next congress in 1904, to be held in Amsterdam.[3]

The Amsterdam Congress's debate on the immigration issue began in a commission established on the question. Morris Hillquit of the American Socialist Party presented a resolution targeting "workers of backward races (Chinese, Negroes, etc.)" and called for the International to oppose such immigration. A majority of the commission strongly disagreed, however, and approved instead a resolution condemning "all legislation designed to prevent emigration."

When the commission's counterposed resolutions came to the plenary late in the congress, it became clear that time constraints would prevent a proper debate. It was therefore decided to hold the question over for a more extensive discussion at the following international congress, before which it would be studied further.

Prior to the Stuttgart Congress of 1907, the American Socialist Party submitted a resolution that called on the International "to combat with all means at their command the willful importation of cheap foreign labor calculated to destroy labor organizations, to lower the standard of living of the working class, and to retard the ultimate realization of socialism." Although this resolution did not openly call for immigration restrictions, such prohibitions were implied.

That perspective was answered by the majority of the Stuttgart Congress immigration commission, which opposed all laws to exclude immigrants, terming these "in conflict with the principle of proletarian solidarity."

The debate on this question in the plenary was particularly sharp. Calls for immigration restrictions were advanced by Hillquit and several other delegates presenting openly racist views toward Asian and Black immigrants. Numerous delegates, however, responded heatedly, rejecting racial prejudice and expressing solidarity with immigrants as fellow workers. In studying these debates now, readers should keep in mind that the word "coolie"—rejected today as derogatory—was widely used and generally accepted at the time as a synonym for unskilled Chinese laborers.

Although the votes on these resolutions in both the commission and the plenary were not recorded in the minutes, the decisive defeat of the opportunist motion marked a victory for left-wing forces within the socialist movement. At the same time, together with the analogous debate on colonialism seen in the previous chapter, what was becoming increasingly apparent was the emergence of an unbridgeable divide within the socialist movement, foreshadowing the split that was to occur following 1914.

The Immigration Debate at the 1904 Amsterdam Congress

Proposed Resolutions

Commission Majority Resolution

The Congress declares that immigrant workers are the victims of the capitalist system, which often forces them to emigrate so as to painfully secure their existence and liberty.

Immigrant workers are often used to replace workers on strike, resulting occasionally in bloody conflicts between workers of different nationalities.

The Congress condemns all legislation designed to prevent emigration.

It declares that propaganda to enlighten emigrants attracted artificially by capitalist entrepreneurs through false information, is absolutely essential.

It is convinced that, owing to socialist propaganda and workers' organization, immigrants will, after a time, be won to the side of the organized workers of the countries of emigration and will demand legal wages.

The Congress further declares that it is useful for socialist representatives in parliament to demand that, through tight and effective measures, governments seek to control the numerous abuses that immigration gives rise to. Socialists in parliament should also propose legislative reforms so that migrant workers acquire political and civil rights in countries of emigration as rapidly as possible, with their rights restored as soon as they return to their countries of origin, or that the various countries ensure immigrants the same rights through reciprocity agreements.

The Congress urges socialist parties and trade union federations to work more vigorously than they have done thus far to spread propaganda among the immigrant workers concerning the organization of workers and international solidarity.

Commission Minority Resolution

Fully considering the dangers connected with the immigration of foreign workingmen, inasmuch as it brings on a reduction of wages and furnishes the material for strikebreakers, occasionally also for bloody conflicts between workingmen, the Congress declares:

That under the influence and agitation from socialist and trade union quarters, the immigrants will gradually rank themselves on the side of the native workers and demand the same wages that the latter demand. Therefore, the Congress condemns all legislative enactment that forbids or hinders the immigration of foreign workingmen whom misery forces to emigrate.

In further consideration of the fact that workers of backward races (Chinese, Negroes, etc.) are often imported by capitalists in order to keep down the native workers by means of cheap labor, and that this cheap labor, which constitutes a willing object of exploitation, lives in an ill-concealed state of slavery, the Congress declares that the Social Democracy is bound to combat with all its energy the application of this means, which serves to destroy the organization of labor, and thereby to hamper the progress and the eventual realization of socialism.

Plenary Debate

Manuel Ugarte (Argentina, reporter): Immigration has presently taken on dimensions that undoubtedly pose a risk for specific countries. In spite of this, the working class did not take the narrow-minded standpoint that workers should remain in their countries but rather claimed workers' right to make the whole world their homeland.

Nevertheless, the phenomenon of induced mass immigration and emigration needs to be assessed. Some governments provoke artificial emigration by masses of the population through restricting to the utmost the political freedom of working people, or through making their economic existence impossible. Other governments promote mass emigration from the imperialist countries in order to send them to parts of the world with the aim of securing new domains. But none of these governments ask about the conditions under which mass emigration will occur: about how people will be crammed aboard ships by exploitative shipping companies, about what exploitation and subjugation they will face in their new countries.

Mass migration can be fought, however, only by thoroughgoing reforms. That is why we now have to think about measures that will give emigrants humane treatment along their path of suffering, such as secure protection against fraud. In order to protect their rights, immigrants also have to be naturalized immediately without losing citizenship in their old homeland. It is necessary to work energetically to defend the rights of immigrants in their new homeland and to prevent this leading to a depression of wages in these countries.

Morris Hillquit (United States) argues for the resolution of the American, Dutch, and British colonies' delegations [the immigration commission minority resolution]. All these countries are compelled to make a distinction between workers of civilized and uncivilized countries, between workers who are engaged in the class struggle—or at least are in the process of developing class consciousness—and those who do not yet have the slightest precondition for this.

The difference between the two resolutions is in the last sentence of the resolution and applies to the employment of colored men. In America, Canada, and Australia, we feel the competition from Chinese coolies. They are imported by the tens of thousands in order to destroy trade union organizations. That is why American unions promulgated a ban on importing Chinese. This measure can be called reactionary, but it is absolutely necessary to keep the coolies away if we do not want to destroy the trade unions.

Nicholas Klein (United States) protested the Hillquit amendment, in the name of half the American delegation. This amendment will bring discord into the working class, contradicting the slogan "Workers of all countries, unite!" The coolies are people too—workers—and they have the same rights as anyone else. Competition within the workforce does not come just from the Chinese, but also from Hungarians, Poles, and Russians.

Fritz Paeplow (Germany): International solidarity should not be seen in this fashion. Workers in countries where life is cheap cannot easily compete with workers from countries where life is dear. That's why the situation of German workers is made considerably worse by the immigration of Italian workers. Despite this, it is impossible for me to vote for Hillquit's motion, which goes too far. The trade unions in America would have done better to open their doors to foreign workers, so that they could jointly struggle for improved working conditions.

Keir Hardie (Britain): The British could not vote for any of the resolutions presented here and proposed not to discuss this important question any more, time being too short. The question of immigration and emigration should be dealt with in detail at the next congress. The International Socialist Bureau should prepare the question to be discussed there.

The Immigration Debate at the 1907 Stuttgart Congress

Proposed Resolutions

Argentine SP Resolution

The Congress declares that propaganda is absolutely necessary in order to check the emigration artificially fostered by governments for the benefit of the capitalist class and to the disadvantage of the working class, which is misled by false information as to a prosperity that does not exist.

The Congress declares that parliamentary representatives of the [Socialist] Party should work to reform legislation so that naturalized citizens in the countries of immigration can choose the citizenship they prefer on returning to their native country.

American SP Resolution

It is the duty of socialists and organized workers of all countries:

1. To advise and assist the bona fide workingmen immigrants in their first struggles on the new soil; to educate them to the principles of socialism and trade unionism; to receive them in their respective organizations; and to enlist them in the labor movement of the country of their adoption as speedily as possible.

2. To counteract the efforts of misleading representations of capitalist promoters by the publication and wide circulation of truthful reports on

the labor conditions of their respective countries, especially through the medium of the International Bureau.

3. To combat with all means at their command the willful importation of cheap foreign labor calculated to destroy labor organizations, to lower the standard of living of the working class, and to retard the ultimate realization of socialism.

4. To seek to procure and protect for all residents in the United States, regardless of race or nativity, full and equal civil and political rights, including the right to naturalization for all and admission on equal terms to the benefits of the schools and other public institutions.

5. To promote the enrollment of workers of alien race or nativity in the political and industrial organization of the working class and the cultivation of a mutual good understanding and fraternal relations between them and the mass of native white workers.

6. By all means to further the assimilation of all such alien elements on a basis of common interest as wageworkers and to rebuke all appeals to racial, national, or religious prejudice against or among them.

The Congress calls upon the socialist representatives in the parliaments of the various countries to introduce legislation along the general lines laid down in this resolution, as well as legislation tending to secure to immigrated workingmen full civil and political rights in the countries of their adoption as speedily as possible. The Congress leaves it to the various national organizations to apply the principles herein announced to the specific needs and conditions of their respective countries.

Belgian Workers Party Amendment to American SP resolution:

Considers as ineffectual and dangerous all measures that would have as a consequence removing bonafide immigrant workers.

Urges socialist members of parliament to demand equality of rights for immigrant workers in matters of social legislation.

Urges the unions to multiply the issuance of transfer papers giving immigrant workers equality of rights in the organizations they will have to enter.

Bund Resolution[4]

I

The congress expresses the conviction:

1. That immigration today is a result of the prevailing capitalist form of production, brought about by causes that are closely linked to the whole modern economic order.

2. That its sometimes-abnormal development is determined on the one hand by political, religious, and national persecution in the countries of emigration; on the other hand, by the appeal addressed by governments and employers to surplus labor forces for purposes of exploitation, and by turning the transport of immigrants into an autonomous capitalist enterprise.

3. That given such close ties between immigration and the prevailing capitalist order, any attempt to put an end to immigration through restrictive laws will be useless and, by its very nature, reactionary.

4. That legislation by capitalist governments against immigration does not improve the situation of workers, does not in any way limit capitalist exploitation, and influences in the most harmful way the fate of workers who see emigration as a refuge from hunger, persecution, and pogroms. While legislation against immigration does not achieve its stated goal, at the same time it obstructs the class consciousness of workers, distances the proletariat from the class struggle, sows discord among workers, and creates an atmosphere encouraging racial and national struggles.

Based on these considerations, the Congress declares itself against any laws limiting emigration and immigration and urges all socialist parties to fight energetically against such laws and to explain to the proletariat their true character.

II

To combat the unfortunate consequences of the disproportionate entry of workers into the countries of immigration, the Congress recommends that all socialist parties and workers' organizations fight energetically to obtain a normal working day in all branches of industry, to regularize wages, to fight against all methods resorted to by governments and employers to attract immigrants, and to demand that immigrants be able to obtain the right of citizenship as soon as possible.

At the same time, socialist parties of the countries of emigration and immigration demand that information offices for immigrants be set up at the expense of the government, with the participation of the trade unions, and that an international agreement be established to protect immigrants and to regulate companies and agencies responsible for their transport.

Finally, the Congress, firmly convinced that the proletariat of all countries and nationalities is capable of fully understanding the key importance of solidarity and community of interests, vigorously rejects the shortsighted policy of many labor organizations that gives no consideration to immigrant workers and differentiates between workers of various races and nationalities.

The Congress considers it a duty of all socialist parties and workers' organizations in countries of immigration to do their utmost to facilitate the entry of immigrant workers into their organizations and to assist in the widest possible dissemination of socialist ideas among them.

Commission Debate

Manuel Ugarte (Argentina): The Argentine comrades have raised the question of immigration and emigration at this congress for the following reasons: we want to combat only artificial immigration—that is, immigration carried out by capitalist government agencies to obtain cheap labor to compete with organized workers. Our comrades also demand measures against the shipping companies' exploitation of emigrants.

This is not a racial question, and the resolution we must adopt is not aimed against the Chinese or the Japanese. Argentina should be open to all workers. But workers should be advised of the working and living conditions of any country to which they wish to emigrate. . . .

Jules Uhry (France): I have read the American resolution drafted by the Socialist Party in the United States. I believe this resolution is contrary to the fundamental principles of socialism. The Americans demand restrictions on immigration, while workers are going abroad due to economic conditions. The Belgians, Germans, Italians, and Spaniards who have immigrated to France do not have strong class consciousness, but our duty is to raise this consciousness.

We think that the best way of reducing the negative consequences resulting from immigration is propaganda, education, and organization. We cannot replace our unitary slogan of "Proletarians of all countries, unite!" by the declaration: "Proletarians of all countries, expel yourselves!" Far from wanting that, the French delegation believes that socialist deputies of all countries should demand within their respective parliaments the abrogation of laws expelling foreigners and should call for the strict application to immigrants of laws protecting workers. We believe that the bosses who bring in low-paid workers should be forced to pay the difference between this low wage and normal wages.

Victor Kroemer (Australia): Australian workers have won very high wages and a good standard of living. That is why the capitalists have introduced yellow labor. The issue of immigration is therefore of greater importance for Australia than for other countries represented here. Through bringing in Chinese and Japanese workers, the capitalists have tried to reduce wages. White immigrant workers are easily organized, while dark-skinned workers are resistant to organization. This is what has led the Australian Labor Party to impose a White Australia policy against the yellow invasion. Asians are the only ones excluded, as they are unable to become part of the organized working class.

Our workers have no hostility in principle to the Chinese and Japanese, but they are compelled to fight an immigration that is simply a capitalist maneuver to wrest from the workers the advantages they have gained. We believe that such an attitude is not contrary to the principles of socialism. Allowing limited immigration would slow the progress of socialism. We certainly desire a general fraternity of peoples, but to achieve such a goal we must protect the workers of our country, so they are not given over defenseless to capitalism.

Adéodat Compère-Morel (France): . . . Rejecting immigrants in the countries they find themselves in constitutes an antisocialist act. They must be able to share the same advantages as their comrades in the new country have won. . . .

Morris Hillquit (United States): The question of immigration and emigration is a very difficult and serious one. Our resolution in no way infringes on the principle of internationalism, which has always been our guide in the United States. There are several types of immigration. First of all, there is natural immigration, which arises from the very nature of the capitalist economy. For these immigrants we demand full freedom, and we consider it a duty of workers to assist the poor among them.

Another type of immigration must be sharply distinguished from the first. Basically it amounts to capitalism's importation of foreign labor cheaper than that of native-born workers. This threatens the native-born with dangerous competition and usually provides a pool of unconscious strikebreakers. Chinese and Japanese workers play that role today, as does the yellow race in general. While we have absolutely no racial prejudices against the Chinese, we must frankly tell you that they cannot be organized. Only a people well advanced in its historical development, such as the Belgians and Italians in France, can be organized for the class struggle. The Chinese have lagged too far behind to be organized.

Socialism is by no means sentimentalism. A fierce struggle rages between capital and labor, and those who stand against organized labor are our enemy. Do we want to grant privileges to foreign strikebreakers when they are locked in struggle with native-born workers? If we fail to take measures against the importation of Chinese strikebreakers, we will thrust the socialist workers' movement backwards. Our resolution is based on the principle of the class struggle, while the resolution they want to impose on us undermines the principles of this struggle. The American thesis is therefore the most revolutionary, because it alone ensures the development of the labor movement, without holding it back. We do not insist on its every word, but we hope you will adopt a resolution with its general approach.

József Diner-Dénes (Hungary): I cannot accept Comrade Hillquit's point of view. Those countries that cannot be organized today will be organized tomorrow. Moreover, in backward countries this evolution proceeds more rapidly than it did in countries that developed earlier, such as England and Germany. Only ten years ago our Hungarian workers emigrating to America were considered unorganizable. Today, only a few years later, they are being organized and are inspired with the spirit of socialism.

You want to erect protective barriers around the workers. This will land you in the same fiasco as the tariff-building efforts of the capitalists. If the wage question was merely one of supply and demand, we would have to oppose the importation of agricultural machinery, since it has replaced more workers than the Japanese and Chinese, especially in the Eastern European countries.

We must permit completely free immigration and emigration. A great many American workers are wage conscious but not yet imbued with proletarian class consciousness. We must of course fight against the abuses that stem from the mass importation of workers for the capitalists' benefit, but through explanation and organization. A good method would be to press for the establishment of a minimum wage—where possible through political means, otherwise through trade union struggle. [*Enthusiastic applause*]

Mark Lucas (South Africa): For my part, I support Hillquit's point of view. We are not enemies of the Chinese as a race, but as strikebreakers. We must stop the importation of low-paid workers; otherwise our unions will be broken. On the question of the immigration of workers who are organizable, we accept all the resolutions of the Socialist International.

Charles Rappoport (France): . . . We cannot accept Hillquit's talk of predestined strikebreakers. So long as a worker has not acted as a strike-breaker, we treat him as a comrade. We too want to take a stand against immigration organized by the capitalists to break contracts, but not by fighting against the workers involved.

Nicolae Dumitru Cocea (Romania): Two types of immigration have been mentioned here: natural immigration and artificial immigration. There is a third type, which is due to the mass expulsion of workers through government measures. Romania falls into this category. There are over a hundred thousand Jews who are deprived of all rights. Any police officer can come and take measures against them. They can be driven from their homes and left abandoned in the countryside.

These acts of violence, this intolerable situation, is carried out by the Romanian government against foreign socialists and against native socialists who demand the intervention by representatives of the people and parliaments against this forced emigration. If Romanian citizens can be expelled by their own government, then other governments can expel Romanian citizens. Where will these unfortunate people go?

I bring this to the attention of our friends in Hungary and Austria in particular.

Wilhelm Ellenbogen (Austria): Two opposite trends have emerged in this discussion. Some speak for the interests of the country of immigration and others for those of the emigrants. No reconciliation appears possible between the two points of view. That is a mistake. But we must combine them and make provisions for both sides. This is best done by excluding from the outset measures unacceptable to socialists, such as guildlike regulations and discriminatory laws.

I hope Comrade Hillquit will not be offended, but I cannot accept his resolution because it is not clearly formulated. We should avoid distinctions such as those between "natural" and "unnatural" immigration, which are slippery and hard to define. However, we do have a number of positive measures, in which the main tasks fall to the trade unions. The unions should reach out to the countries of emigration and educate the emigrants there, as the German trade unions have done in such an exemplary fashion. They must also try to prevent the export of strikebreakers. Most importantly, the trade unions of the country of immigration must make special efforts to attract the immigrant workers. Here I find it most regrettable that many American trade unions make it difficult for immigrants to join.

Social legislation poses a second set of tasks. The proposal of Diner-Dénes to demand a minimum wage should be supplemented with one for a limit on the hours of work. We must also demand supervision of recruitment and, above all, regulation of conditions on the emigration ships. A requirement of a certain amount of air space per person in the cabins would make Chinese immigration in its worst form impossible, since their transportation would no longer produce a profit. . . .

Kato Tokijiro (Japan): As the representative of the Japanese socialists, I must take the floor on this very important question. When the Americans excluded us from California they gave two reasons: first, that Japanese workers were depressing the wages and living standards of the indigenous workers, and second, that we were taking away their opportunity to work.[5] I disagree with this. This is done not only by the Japanese, but also by the Italians, Slovaks, Jews, and so forth. So why is it that only the Japanese are being excluded? The race question obviously plays a role here, and the Americans are clearly being influenced by the famous spectacle of the "yellow peril." The history of the United States confirms this opinion. Another factor is that, by talking up the dangers of Japanese immigration, the American capitalists want to appeal to certain instincts among the workers.

The Japanese are under the heel of capitalism just as much as other peoples. It is only dire need that drives them from their homeland to earn their livelihood in a foreign land. It is the duty of socialists to welcome these poor brothers, to defend them, and together with them to fight capitalism. Proletarians of all countries, unite! The founders of socialism, above all Karl Marx, did not address themselves to one single country but to all humanity. Internationalism is inscribed on our banner. It would be a slap in the face of socialism if you were to exclude the poor, exploited Japanese. [*Enthusiastic, prolonged applause*]

Julius Hammer (United States, Socialist Labor Party): There is no middle ground on this question of immigration and emigration. Either you support immigration restriction, or energetically combat it. Hillquit's resolution is an attempt at compromise that misses the mark. I especially oppose its third point that envisages possible restrictions on the immigration of Chinese and Japanese workers. This is completely anti-socialist. Legal restriction of immigration must be rejected. Nothing can be gained for socialism through legislative action, or through collaboration with the bourgeois parties.

The Japanese and Chinese could be very effectively organized. They are not as unskilled as you might suppose. They are becoming quite well acquainted with capitalism and are learning how to fight it. I ask that you not approve any legal restrictions on immigration and emigration. We must create a great nation of the exploited.

Malecki (Poland): I too am in favor of freedom of immigration. Workers who leave their countries do so to escape death by hunger. If American workers want to prevent the migration of cheap labor in the interests of the capitalists, they should fight for a minimum wage. The American resolution is due to the fact that the unions in that country are infected with the bourgeois spirit.

Kahan (Britain): When Hillquit calls for the prohibition of strikebreakers lacking consciousness, I agree with him. But when he wants to limit voluntary immigration, I declare myself his adversary, since his motion constitutes an attack on the freedom of movement. It would also be applying a method of bourgeois education, aimed at dividing the workers. Proletarians constitute a class that we cannot divide. We must also speak out against all distinctions between the races.

I am ashamed to say that at this moment it is England—the classic country of trade unionism—where the bosses look for strikebreakers to break strikes in other countries. This proves that in reality there is no such thing as inferior races. Strikebreakers can be found in all countries, and the speech by the delegate from Japan showed us that Japanese workers are not hostile to organization and that they agree with the principles of the International. They are our brothers.

Giovanni Valär (Italy): . . . We cannot think of limiting immigration, a consequence of capitalist society, and we must take measures to prevent results harmful to the proletariat—such as those taken by the German unions in attempting to organize Italian immigrant workers—and to prevent these workers from rendering the expected services to international capitalism. It is the creation of unions and the holding of workers' assemblies that can remedy the consequences of immigration. Workers' legislation must be improved and made available and applicable to immigrants

I warn the congress against the measures of the American trade unions in preventing foreign workers from entering the unions, thereby pushing them to become strikebreakers. We are against immigration restrictions, because we know that the whip of hunger is stronger than the law.

Willem Hubertus Vliegen (Netherlands): . . . Immigration must be free. Wherever there is a high level of immigration, wages are generally better in comparison to countries where immigration is closed off. It has not yet been shown that immigration depresses wages. Rather, in countries with a high level of immigration, wages improve for those workers remaining. In Holland, for example, many agricultural workers emigrated, and those remaining saw their wages rise.

Oddly, the American East is open, but the West—where Japanese and Chinese go—is closed. What can be the reason for this phenomenon other than racial hatred? Russians are admitted, but those from Asia are rejected. If this is not a question of race, what is it? Why treat Japanese as an inferior race? . . .

Fritz Paeplow (Germany): We believe that emigration and immigration can be subject to wise limitation. We therefore support the Hillquit resolution. . . .

We are ready to accept foreign immigrants, infusing them with our culture and teaching them of our experience, but we must guard against the mass importation of them. In Germany we are faced with the danger of the importation of coolies. Our big shipping companies have begun to bring in such labor power, with the Chinese being sent to our mines and to work as farm laborers. . . .

I oppose the restrictive measures of the American trade unions, but we Germans cannot accept a resolution rejecting all limitations.

Plenary Debate

Wilhelm Ellenbogen (Germany, reporter): . . . The question that concerns us at this moment is one of the biggest problems posed by capitalism. Modern immigration surpasses in intensity and extent the great immigrations of peoples in ancient times. It involves entire generations and uproots them from their native soil. It transplants entire nations to foreign countries. Sometimes it destroys original civilizations and creates new nations and cultures.

The principal cause of this change is the insatiable desire of capitalism to enrich itself. Organized workers raised to consciousness by socialism demand a greater part of the product of their labor. This demand, which is a reduction of the rate of profit, is one that capitalism cannot accept in the long run. Profits must again be raised, and the workers must fight on behalf of their own brethren. The power of their organizations must again be destroyed. The tendency to bring in poorly paid workers belongs to the essence of capitalism, as well as the exploitation of all other economic and social phenomena that are the products of contemporary society. The ruin of the old agrarian economy drives workers and small peasants from the country due to hunger and disease. . . .

The current congress, which represents the socialist ideas of all countries, does not imitate capitalism's example. Our duty can be expressed in the following formula: we must protect both native workers and immigrant workers. If we protect only native workers, we sacrifice millions of immigrants to the lust of capitalism. If we protect only immigrants, we destroy the organizations that the native workers have created through years of long and difficult labor. It is clear that Social Democracy, seeking to bring about this protection in practice, cannot resort to laws of exclusion. [*"Bravo!"*] You will notice that this principle is formulated in a number of parts of the text of our resolution: no exclusion. Unfortunately, there are some workers' organizations that have tried to stop the immigration of workers belonging to a different race than they do. I do not believe that those who do this are socialists.

Everything that has been said about the inferiority of certain nations does not stand up to historical evolution. We have said that once a nation could breathe, once it broke away from ancient constraints and made contact with modern civilization, then we can no longer exclude anyone from the possibility of raising themselves up today.

On the other hand, workers, like nations, must not interpret international solidarity in a colorless way, as an incitement to renounce their own nationality. On the contrary, workers of all nations have the right to love and show enthusiasm for the cultures that their own nations have created. [*"Bravo!"*] They will better guard their own originality and conserve the essence of their civilization, while favoring the interests of the whole. But they will also show deference to the character of other nations, considering it a crime to keep down other nations that aspire to a higher degree of culture.

I would also like to say something else: it is not always possible to determine precisely what is superior and inferior in the evolution of a nation. There are some nations considered very highly developed that were beaten by races considered backward, from which it will take them several years to recover. It has finally been discovered that the despised race is highly developed enough that a number of European nations can now hold it up as an example. . . .

Comrades, your nice speeches and our fine resolutions will mean nothing if we do not infuse ourselves with the spirit of solidarity and international brotherhood of all those who suffer under the yoke of capitalism, inspired by the well-known call of the Communist Manifesto. Not only must you vote for the resolution, but also work to assure its application. [*Long applause*]

Morris Hillquit (United States): . . . The basis of the class struggle within every country is the organization of the native working class. Within each country we make a distinction between the organized working class and strikebreakers. We cannot tolerate strikebreakers from our own country, nor can we allow them to come from other countries. That is why we Americans have up to now been opposed to the immigration of strikebreakers. In calling for immigration prohibitions, we have by necessity done so with regard to immigration from the East. It was therefore not a racial struggle in reality. Measures were taken not against Italians and other Europeans, but against immigrants who are unorganizable.

We recognize that from a socialist point of view, exceptional measures against a class or a nation are unacceptable. We have tried to overcome very serious difficulties according to the method we deem appropriate. . . .

Adopted Resolution

The Congress declares:

Immigration and emigration of workers are phenomena as inseparable from the substance of capitalism as unemployment, overproduction, and underconsumption of the workers; they are frequently one of the means to reduce the share of the workers in the product of labor, and at times they assume abnormal dimensions through political, religious, and national persecutions.

The Congress does not consider exceptional measures of any kind, economic or political, [to be] the means for removing any danger that may arise to the working class from immigration and emigration, since such measures are fruitless and reactionary: especially not the restriction of the freedom of migration and the exclusion of foreign nations and races.

At the same time, the Congress declares it to be the duty of organized workers to protect themselves against the lowering of their standard of living, which frequently results from the mass import of unorganized workers. The Congress declares it to be their duty to prevent the import and export of strikebreakers.

The Congress recognizes the difficulties that in many cases confront the workers of the countries of a more advanced stage of capitalist development through the mass immigration of unorganized workers accustomed to a lower standard of living and coming from countries of prevalently agricultural and domestic civilization, and also the dangers that confront them from certain forms of immigration.

But the Congress sees no proper solution of these difficulties in the exclusion of definite nations or races from immigration, a policy that is besides in conflict with the principle of proletarian solidarity.

The Congress, therefore, recommends the following measures:

I

For the countries of immigration:

1. Prohibition of the export and import of such workers who have entered into a contract that deprives them of the liberty to dispose of their labor power and wages.

2. Legislation shortening the workday, fixing a minimum wage, regulating the sweating system [subcontracting sweatshops] and house industry, and providing for strict supervision of sanitary and dwelling conditions.

3. Abolition of all restrictions that exclude definite nationalities or races from the right of sojourn in the country and from the political and economic rights of the natives, or make the acquisition of these rights more difficult for them. It also demands the greatest latitude in the laws of naturalization.

4. For the trade unions of all countries, the following principles shall have universal application in connection with it:

   (a) Unrestricted admission of immigrant workers to the trade unions of all countries.

   (b) Facilitating the admission of members by means of fixing reasonable admission fees.

   (c) Free transfer from the organizations of one country to those of the other upon the discharge of the membership obligations towards the former organization.

   (d) The making of international trade union agreements for the purpose of regulating these questions in a definite and proper manner, and enabling the realization of these principles on an international scale.

5. Support of the trade unions of those countries from which the immigration is chiefly recruited.

II

For the countries of emigration:

1. Active propaganda for trade unionism.

2. Enlightenment of the workers and the public at large on the true conditions of labor in the countries of immigration.

3. Concerted action on the part of the trade unions of all countries in all matters of labor immigration and emigration.

4. In view of the fact that emigration of workers is often artificially stimulated by railway and steamship companies, land speculators, and other swindling concerns through false and lying promises to workers, the Congress demands:

Control of the steamship agencies and emigration bureaus, and legal and administrative measures against them, in order to prevent emigration from being abused in the interests of such capitalist concerns.

III

Regulation of the system of transportation, especially on ships. Employment of inspectors with discretionary power over who should be selected by the organized workers of the countries of emigration and immigration. Protection for the newly arrived immigrants, in order that they may not become the victims of capitalist exploiters.

In view of the fact that the transport of emigrants can only be regulated on an international basis, the Congress directs the International Socialist Bureau to prepare suggestions for the regulation of this question, which shall deal with the conditions, arrangements, and supplies of the ships, the air space to be allowed for each passenger as a minimum, and shall lay special stress that the individual emigrants contract for their passage directly with the transportation companies and without intervention of middlemen. These suggestions shall be communicated to the various socialist parties for the purpose of legislative application, and adaptation, as well as for the purposes of propaganda.

4.

The Debate on Women’s Suffrage

Introductory Note on the Women's Suffrage Debate

In the early twentieth century, women lacked the right to vote almost everywhere. New Zealand became the first country to grant women the ballot in parliamentary elections in 1893, although it took another quarter century for women to win the right to stand for election to parliament. Within Europe, the only country to have granted full suffrage rights to women by 1907 was Finland—then part of the Russian Empire—which obtained this right in the context of the 1905 revolution that shook the tsarist regime. The lack of voting rights reflected women's status in society as a whole. Excluded almost entirely from political and social rights, women were largely confined to the family household.

Yet capitalism itself was beginning to change this situation, drawing women more and more into the industrial workforce as a source of cheap labor. By doing so, it unintentionally began to break down elements of women's traditional role and bring masses of them into social life. In Britain in 1907 there were already 150,000 women belonging to trade unions; in Germany the figure was 120,000.

The increasing number of female workers strengthened the struggle for women's emancipation as well as the possibility to connect this battle more closely to the working-class fight against capitalism. This new reality increased women's social weight and potential power, posing more sharply the need for the working-class and socialist movements to champion the fight for women's rights.

* * *

By 1907 the socialist movement already had a tradition of giving support to the fight for women's full political, economic, and social emancipation.

The first major Marxist analysis of women's oppression was August Bebel's *Woman and Socialism*, which appeared in 1879. Five years later, Frederick Engels's *The Origin of the Family, Private Property, and the State* was published. These two works guided generations of socialist activists, rooting the oppression of women squarely in capitalism and class society, and pointing out that the road to women's emancipation lay through the proletarian struggle for socialism. Based on this perspective, the socialist movement took a firm position opposed to women's oppression, in particular the denial of full citizenship rights such as the right to vote.

Yet alongside the Marxist movement's open support for women's rights were important weaknesses in its day-to-day conduct. Socialists often failed to see fully the centrality of the fight for women's emancipation within the overall proletarian struggle. As a result, a tendency existed among many Marxists to stand aside from concrete struggles around this issue, seeing them as diversions from the broader working-class movement and viewing women's emancipation as simply a by-product of socialism.

Prior to 1907, the Second International had adopted a number of resolutions on the question. For instance, at the 1891 congress several female delegates put forward a resolution calling for socialist and labor parties "to affirm energetically in their programs the complete equality of the two sexes and to demand that women be granted the same political and civil rights as men, and the repeal of all laws placing women outside public rights." An 1893 resolution was directed toward establishing protective legislation for working women. The Amsterdam Congress of 1904 adopted a resolution on women's suffrage: "In the struggles that the proletariat wages for the conquest of universal, equal, direct, and secret suffrage to parliament and municipal councils, socialist parties must put forward the demand for women's suffrage. This demand must be maintained as a principle in agitation and defended energetically."[1]

Despite these formally adopted international resolutions, however, most socialist parties tended to downplay women's suffrage and women's rights in general, refusing to prioritize the issue. This political stance was exacerbated by—and contributed to—the small number of women in the socialist movement and the minimal role they were assigned, with their efforts and capabilities consistently underestimated and undervalued.

Recalling that history, Clara Zetkin later stated: "Women's activity was regarded more or less as that of a servant to the party or union, and its true significance as a meaningful factor in the proletarian struggle for liberation was not recognised."[2]

To address this situation, women within the socialist movement began to organize collectively to assert their power and advance the struggle for women's rights. The result was the creation of the Socialist Women's Movement.

The roots of this movement began in Germany. A socialist women's organization was established there in the 1890s as a product of necessity. At the time, legal restrictions in Germany prevented women's involvement in political parties and activities, including membership in the Social Democratic Party (SPD). Separate women's structures were thus organized, and beginning in 1900, women in the SPD held annual conferences.

* * *

In 1907, the German Socialist Women's Movement, led by Zetkin, helped organize an international socialist women's conference, to be held on the eve of the Second International's Stuttgart Congress of 1907; this conference took place August 17 and 19. The central political campaign outlined at that meeting was the fight for women's suffrage, with political differences around the issue coming from two directions.

First, representatives of the British Fabian Society and Independent Labour Party advocated support for limited women's suffrage, based on property qualifications, which they viewed as a step forward. This property-qualification provision was supported by some organizations of largely upper-class women that could properly be labeled as "bourgeois feminists."

Secondly, some delegates from Austria supported the position advanced by that country's Social Democratic Party during a recent election campaign. Amid the fight for universal male suffrage in Austria, the party had decided not to make an issue of women's suffrage, seeing it as a diversion from what it considered the more important fight.

Both positions were rejected by Zetkin and the majority of the delegates, who approved, by a vote of 47 to 11, a resolution proposed by the German delegation calling for an international campaign for universal women's suffrage.

The resolution of the women's conference was then brought into the Second International's Stuttgart Congress, where it was debated first in a commission and then in the full plenary. In the commission, a motion by Victor Adler to largely uphold the policy of the Austrian party was defeated by 9 votes for and 12 against. In the plenary, the women's-suffrage resolution was adopted with a single opposing vote, coming from the representative of the Fabian Society.

The creation of the Socialist Women's Movement had an important and lasting impact on the worldwide struggle for women's rights. The most well-known example of this impact came out of the next international socialist women's conference, held in 1910, which issued a call for the establishment of International Women Workers' Day. The date of March 8 was soon settled upon. Over a century later, International Women's Day is commemorated by millions around the world, although few are aware of its socialist origins.

The Women's Suffrage Debate at the 1907 Stuttgart Congress

Commission Debate

Victor Adler (Austria): The success of our latest electoral struggle is due in particular to the spirit of sacrifice, to the discipline and intelligence of the members of the [socialist] women's leagues. [*"Very good!"*] They waged the battle together with us and were victorious together with us. They did more. They bowed voluntarily to the tactical needs of our struggle and had the merit of understanding the difficulties of the situation. They showed us the way. Their situation was very difficult.

The bourgeois women were holding meetings in favor of women's suffrage, at a time when the question of male suffrage had not yet been resolved, and these women encouraged our comrades to participate in their movement. But our women comrades understood that their place was alongside us, because our cause is a common one: the cause of all proletarians. [*"Bravo!"*] Our women came here and they stood before the delegates of all countries. They do not ask that we thank them or pay tribute to them. Neither do they merit the criticism of comrades from other countries. These are criticisms emanating from comrades whom I personally appreciate, but who do not understand the situation we face in Austria. [*Movement in the audience*]

For this reason, we want to insert in the resolution something saying that it is up to organizations in each country to choose the appropriate method to fight for universal women's suffrage.

Clara Zetkin (Germany): . . . We have not criticized the Austrian women at all. It was stated expressly that our resolution had no intention of criticizing, and that we did not want to play the part of pawns. What it gave was an indication of the electoral struggle to come. [*"Very good!"*]

The question we have been discussing is whether it was really necessary to discard women's right to vote. From that point of view, we are certainly permitted to hold a different point of view from that of Comrade Adler.

I believe that the international congress has the duty of indicating general directions, of setting forth principles. Otherwise it is simply an assembly of friends, lacking any importance as to the activity of international Social Democracy. For us, maintaining our principles is also a question of principle and not of tactics. We will not abandon our ideas in face of a struggle, and without a struggle.

Adler: Comrade Zetkin said correctly that the congress should set principles according to which the parties have to proceed; otherwise its meetings would have no purpose. For this reason I accept everything in the resolution related to principles. But all that has nothing to do with the practical implementation of our principles. I believe that each country should determine—with full knowledge and consciousness, as well as full responsibility—*when* to undertake the struggle for the principles adopted here. [*"Very good!"*] I propose that this idea be formulated in a special passage. If Comrade Zetkin thinks it better not to add this sentence, I can simply say that her attitude won't change anything. [*"Very good!"*] So accept our proposal, and you'll show that you understand the fact that the political conjuncture in each country creates what is possible and desirable at any given moment. [*"Bravo!"*]

Madeleine Pelletier (France): I cannot accept the Austrian proposal. It tends to permit men to set aside votes for women for the sake of expediency. I am opposed to a text that gives us platonic satisfaction and nothing more.

Adelheid Popp (Austria): Comrade Zetkin stated that we were not criticized. That's wrong. We were criticized in Mannheim,[3] where I was not permitted to speak in order to explain our situation. We hold the view that it is not just socialist women who have the duty of fighting for women's suffrage and for suffrage in general, but Social Democratic parties as a whole.

We believe that the cause of women's suffrage will make great progress if the commission will ask of the congress that large demonstrations of all Social Democrats be organized in every country, at a given moment, in favor of women's suffrage.

Kathleen B. Kough (Britain, Social Democratic Federation): I propose the following amendment:

"The International Socialist Congress recognizes that it cannot prescribe for each country the exact date in which to begin a movement to win women's suffrage."

I nevertheless state that when such a movement is begun in a certain country, it must be continued in conformity with socialist principles, that is, in favor of universal suffrage for men and women.

Zetkin: It seems to me that we're losing the object of the debate. We do not at all wish to reissue a statement of principle in favor of votes for women. What is at issue, rather, is to take a step toward winning this vote. [*"Bravo!"*] The question is therefore: What path are we to follow?

Our opinion is that the struggle for women's suffrage cannot be separated from the political struggles of the male proletariat. We oppose those who want women's suffrage to be separated from future struggles for tactical reasons.

Certainly our political education is not so backward as to demand that every country make votes for women the cornerstone of the struggle at all times. That will depend on the historical development of the various countries. But we criticize the tactical decision of consistently putting women's suffrage in one's pocket ahead of time and without a struggle. We do this so as not to undermine international solidarity. Such solidarity does not consist of always elevating what a party does as an example, but trying to put it back on track.

I ask you above all to accept the part of the resolution that condemns limited suffrage for women. That is a declaration of principle that we stand on.

Margaret McMillan (Britain, Independent Labour Party): I want to justify the attitude of the English women who are fighting for limited suffrage for women. Women who make this sacrifice for the cause should be recognized as citizens fighting for a high goal, and it should not be said here that they have sold out to wealthy women. Keir Hardie, who is certainly recognized as a valiant champion of the proletariat, thinks that granting suffrage to British women under current conditions would give the vote to 80 percent of women. The stakes are well worth the battle.

C. N. L. Shaw (Britain): It would be a very great misfortune if we accepted limited suffrage. I do not at all agree that under current law 80 percent of women would benefit. At best we could estimate the percentage as one-third.

Plenary Debate

Clara Zetkin (Germany, reporter): . . . The proletariat has a vital interest in the political equality of women and must participate in the conquest of these rights. This struggle arouses the masses of women and helps raise them to class consciousness. Recognizing women's right to vote thus prepares proletarian women for participation in the class struggle. At the same time, women need to be awakened, organized, and educated with the same fervor as has been given to the organization and education of the male proletariat.

As long as women are deprived of public rights, they will be viewed as powerless, as a force whose influence will not be judged at its real value. In parliamentary life it is the ballot that has value. Shortsighted men who view the political struggle only within the framework of ballots and mandates consider the efforts to awaken proletarian women to class consciousness to be a pastime and luxury that Social Democracy can indulge in only when it possesses an excess of time, energy, and money. These people overlook the proletariat's urgent class interest in developing the class struggle among women, so that proletarian women stand alongside their brothers. The moment women are politically emancipated and have the right to vote, this interest will become clear to even the most shortsighted men in our ranks. At that point a race will begin by all parties to try and win the votes of proletarian women, who constitute the majority of the female sex. The socialist parties must therefore make the necessary efforts to overcome the bourgeois parties in the area of women's education. . . .

In these days of intensified class struggle, the question arises as to what type of suffrage socialists should fight for. A few years ago, this question would have been unnecessary. We would have answered simply: "Votes for women." At that time, limited suffrage would have been seen as insufficient, but nevertheless as a step along the road toward women's emancipation. Today such a conception is no longer possible. Socialist parties today must declare firmly that they fight only for the unrestricted suffrage of all women, and that they decisively reject limited suffrage and see it as an infringement of the principle of political equality.

What was previously done instinctively—that is, to reinforce property ownership by introducing limited suffrage—is now done consciously. In breaking down the principled opposition against such suffrage, the bourgeois parties are confronting two situations: the growing internal and external needs of large numbers of bourgeois women forced to fight for their civil rights, together with the growing fear of the political might of the proletariat. In such a situation, the introduction of limited women's suffrage appears as a solution. The proletariat is to pay the cost of maintaining peace between men and women of the propertied classes. The possessing classes see the introduction of limited suffrage as a protective wall against the increasing power of the fighting proletariat. . . .

We regard women's suffrage less as the first stage of the political emancipation of women than as the last stage of the political emancipation of property. Limited suffrage is a privilege of property and not a universal right. It does not emancipate women *because* they are women, but *in spite of* the fact that they are women. Rights are granted to women not as individuals per se, but because of their wealth and income. It thus leaves the great majority of women in a state of dependency, while changing the labels. But the disenfranchisement of proletarian women is a blow against the working class as a whole. It constitutes a type of plural vote for the propertied class and strengthens its political power.

For this reason it is incorrect to consider limited suffrage for women as a practical step toward the political emancipation of proletarian women. On the contrary, limited suffrage reinforces the political power of the propertied class, strengthening the reactionary forces that oppose democratization of the vote for proletarians without distinction of sex. Granting limited suffrage would certainly satisfy bourgeois women, who will stop demanding the extension of their rights to women as a whole. There is not a single country where bourgeois women who have won the right to vote are still fighting for universal women's suffrage.

The more the forces of reaction have recourse to limited suffrage to reduce the growing power of the proletariat, the more it becomes necessary to enlighten proletarian women on the reality of this phenomenon. In short, we must prevent the realization of this reform, which benefits a few, from increasing injustice, which is to the detriment of the masses.

Our fight for votes for women is not a suffragist movement, but a mass movement of the working class. Theoretically and practically, it is an organic part of our whole movement and our socialist program. We must, therefore, not only make constant propaganda for this reform, but must also make it an integral part of the whole electoral effort waged by socialist parties for political democracy. In accordance with this view, the commission decided that all electoral battles must also include the right of women to vote. Proletarian women and proletarian men will be the winners of this common fight. This fact was demonstrated by the election campaign in Finland.[4]

The majority of the commission did not share the opinion that women's suffrage can, for reasons of expediency, be withdrawn without a struggle during a general electoral campaign. The propertied classes oppose democratization of the right to vote, which they view as the end of domination by their class. It is not the character and extent of socialist reforms that determines the outcome of the struggle, but the relationship of power between the exploiters and the exploited. It is not our moderation that leads us to victory, but our power. . . .

The electoral struggle that Social Democracy pursues in favor of women's rights is widening and developing. It uproots old prejudices and shakes up the masses, while creating disunity, uncertainty, and confusion among our enemies. It sharpens the social contradiction between men and women of the ruling classes. This is why it is in the interests of the working class to fight vigorously for the achievement of political equality. We are convinced, therefore, that it is in the class interest of the proletariat and socialist parties to go beyond mere recognition of the principle of women's suffrage and to fight to put this principle into practice.

Saying this does not mean that socialist parties must prematurely initiate an electoral struggle for women's suffrage. Nor does it mean that women's suffrage should constitute the leading issue in every electoral campaign, much less that every electoral campaign must be conducted under the slogan of "Women's suffrage or nothing!" The role that the women's suffrage issue should play depends upon the entire historical conjuncture of each country. Socialist parties must fight for all the reforms in the interests of the proletariat, and they take home whatever they can gain from the propertied classes. What is important is to demand votes for women as a matter of principle and to explain the significance of this reform. We are aware that, in most countries, winning women's suffrage will not occur overnight through such action. But we know that such action prepares the road for future victory.

Socialist women must fight energetically in this campaign for political equality and do their utmost to involve masses of proletarian women in the effort. By doing so, they will demonstrate that it is the masses of women themselves who demand the right to vote, and that proletarian women are willing to use this right. Let us step forward without hesitation to fight for women's suffrage. Doing so will help raise proletarian women to class consciousness, which is of the highest significance for the present and future of the proletariat and its struggle for liberation.

Needed are not patient bearers of the cross or slaves resigned to their fate, but resolute, fighting women. From her bones will arise avengers—children nourished by the ideas in her brain and the passion in her heart; agents who not only will replace those fallen on the battlefield, but whose combative virtues will surpass those of their elders! [*Stormy applause*]

Madeline Pelletier (France): Up until modern times, the woman did not exist outside of her sexuality and materiality. The source of her existence was the man, and without him she was nothing. Women in modern times are tired of this tutelage, and they also want their rights. Natural laws are not insurmountable barriers, and when it's said that we are inferior, one cannot forget that the female sex has been oppressed for millennia. Be that as it may; we have as much value socially as men do. For this reason, we demand votes for women as a weapon in the struggle for proletarian liberation.

Millicent Murby (Britain, Fabian Society): We also support the right to vote, but contrary to the view of Citizen Zetkin, we also accept limited suffrage, as a deposit. It is better to give the hungry half a loaf of bread than none at all. We therefore cannot agree with the passage in the resolution on this point. . . .

Adelheid Popp (Austria, Vienna): When the socialist women of Austria asked the International Socialist Bureau to put the question of women's suffrage on the agenda,[5] we did so because during the recent struggle by the Austrian Social Democracy—which unfortunately did not win votes for women—we had the experience of women who, thanks to the propaganda and agitation of Social Democracy, would not be easy prey for the clerical and reactionary parties. If women were to obtain the right to vote, they could take their place, freely and consciously, alongside the men in the Social Democratic Workers Party. [*"Bravo!"*]

We therefore hope that this congress will not only affirm women's suffrage theoretically, but that all Social Democrats will also fight for this reform, despite the difficulties that the political movement of women creates for the family. The struggle for women's rights must be put forward by the socialist parties of all countries. [*Applause*]

Let us not see the demand for women's suffrage primarily as an issue of women's rights—although we consider it a disgrace that working women and mothers are deprived of basic citizenship. Rather, we firmly believe that this fight strengthens the entire working class. [*"Very good!"*] Social Democracy must not wait until women themselves demonstrate for their rights. We must take the lead in the struggle, because it involves proletarian rights.

I cannot accept the views of Citizen Murby. We rely first of all on our comrades, the socialist men of all countries, who know that this is not a feminist issue but is part of the proletarian struggle. They understand that women's suffrage also strengthens the unionization of proletarian women and increases the political strength of the working class.

Herbert Burrows (Britain): . . . It is wrong to put forward ideas similar to those of Miss Murby. Limited suffrage must be rejected. Miss Murby said that it's better to give the hungry half a loaf than no loaf at all. That comparison is not correct. It would be more accurate to compare a whole loaf to a half loaf that's poisoned. For us socialists, the right to vote is poisoned when it strengthens the possessing class. . . .

Adopted Resolution

The Congress greets with the utmost pleasure the First International Socialist Women's Conference, and expresses its entire solidarity with the demands concerning women's suffrage put forward by it.

The Socialist Party repudiates limited women's suffrage as an adulteration and a caricature of the principle of political equality of the female sex. It fights for the sole living, concrete expression of this principle: namely, universal women's suffrage, which should belong to all women of age and not be conditioned by property, taxation, education, or any other qualification that would exclude members of the laboring classes from the enjoyment of this right. The socialist women shall not carry on this struggle for complete equality in voting rights in alliance with the bourgeois feminists, but in common with the socialist parties, which insist upon women's suffrage as one of the fundamental and most important reforms for the full democratization of the political franchise in general.

It is the duty of the socialist parties of all countries to agitate strenuously for the introduction of universal women's suffrage. Hence, the agitation for the democratization of the franchise to the legislative and administrative bodies, both national and local, must also embrace women's suffrage and must insist upon it, whether it be carried out in parliament or elsewhere. In those countries where the democratization of manhood suffrage has already gone sufficiently far, or is completely realized, the socialist parties must raise a campaign in favor of universal women's suffrage, and in connection with it, of course, put forward all those demands that we have yet to realize in the interest of the full civil rights of the male portion of the proletariat.

Although the International Socialist Congress cannot dictate to any country a particular time at which a suffrage campaign should be commenced, it nevertheless declares that when such a campaign is instituted in any country, it should proceed on the general Social Democratic lines of universal adult suffrage without distinction, and nothing less.

5.

The Debate on Militarism and War

Introductory Note on the Militarism and War Debate

During the mid-nineteenth century, European wars were generally fought by one clique of rulers against another to advance particular dynastic interests and reinforce their power. At the same time, armed conflicts sometimes involved fights for national unification and independence that were part of the era of bourgeois revolutions. Such was the case with the battles for German and Italian national unification, as well as various struggles of oppressed nations and nationalities within the Austro-Hungarian, Ottoman, and Russian Empires.

As the imperialist world system emerged on the eve of the twentieth century, however, wars began to take on a new character. Now, they were increasingly fought by a handful of powers involved in carving up the world, with sharpening conflicts over division of the booty. These conflicts included both wars between capitalist rivals, as well as those between imperialist powers and colonized peoples. Examples of such conflicts were the Spanish-American War of 1898 and the subsequent insurgency in the Philippines, the so-called Boer War in southern Africa that began in 1899, the "Boxer Rebellion" war with China in 1900, and the Russo-Japanese War of 1904–05.

In addition, numerous war threats between rival powers occurred in the two decades before World War I. A potential conflict between France and Britain took place as a result of the Fashoda Incident of 1898, and the Morocco crisis of 1905–06 involved clashing interests of the German and French governments. Subsequently, an even more serious threat of all-out European conflict occurred in 1912–13 during the Balkan Wars.[1]

* * *

By the time of the Second International's Stuttgart Congress in 1907, the socialist movement had acquired considerable experience in war-related questions.

In 1866 the Geneva Congress of the International Workingmen's Association (the First International) adopted a resolution on war and militarism demanding abolition of standing armies and the general arming of the people. The following year, the First International's Lausanne Congress adopted another resolution that supported actions "to achieve the abolition of standing armies and the maintenance of peace" and stressed the connection of that fight with "the emancipation of the working class and its liberation from the power and influence of capital." The Brussels Congress of 1868 also discussed the working-class fight against war, declaring, "The Congress urges the workers to cease work should war break out in their respective countries."[2]

Two years later, the First International took up the Franco-Prussian War of 1870–71, with several addresses drafted by Marx. That conflict was originally seen by the First International as a defensive war by Prussia against attempts by France—then under the rule of Emperor Louis Napoleon III—to prevent German national unification. It quickly became clear, however, that the war originated from the reactionary objectives of the Prussian monarchy to achieve this unification under its own control, masterminded by its main political figure, Otto von Bismarck. As Marx warned, "If the German working class allow the present war to lose its strictly defensive character and to degenerate into a war against the French people, victory or defeat will prove alike disastrous."[3]

The defeat of France in the war, and the prospects of a Prussian occupation of Paris, also led directly to the Paris Commune—the world's first workers' government—in which socialists played a prominent role. "The first decree of the Commune," Marx pointed out with regard to the militarism issue, "was the suppression of the standing army, and the substitution for it of the armed people."[4] That measure was to become a central demand of the world socialist movement.

During the Franco-Prussian War, the German Social Democrats' two Reichstag deputies, August Bebel and Wilhelm Liebknecht, gained international recognition by refusing to vote in favor of war expenditures; both were subsequently imprisoned on the charge of treason. That experience helped lead to a stance by the German Social Democratic

Party of giving "not one person, not one penny" to the capitalist war machine. Socialists presented themselves everywhere as opponents of militarism and standing armies and as advocates of the peaceful resolution of international conflicts. Achieving peace was seen as providing the best conditions for pursuing the working-class struggle for socialism.

The Second International continued this tradition: all but one of its nine congresses between 1889 and 1912 adopted resolutions on militarism and war. No other single question received so much attention.

The founding congress of 1889 adopted a resolution calling for the abolition of standing armies and the general arming of the population through the creation of militias.

The 1891 congress in Brussels featured a debate between Domela Nieuwenhuis from the Netherlands and Wilhelm Liebknecht from Germany. Presenting a resolution on the question by Dutch socialists, Nieuwenhuis claimed that it was necessary to answer the threat of war with revolutionary action. He also called on the congress to "reject the distinction between offensive and defensive wars." In his words:

> It is necessary to fight against militarism, which is one of the methods capitalism uses to maintain its domination. This domination is maintained by bayonets, because when the ranks become intelligent, the bourgeois order is lost. Frederick the Great said that if his soldiers were to think, none would remain in the ranks. The victory of the proletariat will bring universal peace. With courage, energy, and perseverance, wars will not occur. When governments declare war, they are committing a revolutionary act, since the peoples have the right—and even the duty—to respond to it by revolution.

Responding for the German Social Democrats, Liebknecht stated:

> Domela Nieuwenhuis advocates that at the time of the war declaration, the people should carry out a [general] strike. Those who issue this appeal would not have time to carry it out, however, as they would be shot before they could act. It is utopian to believe in the possibility for realizing such an action. . . . With resolutions such as that of Nieuwenhuis, we just make ourselves look ridiculous.

Following the exchange, the congress voted down the Dutch resolution, but Nieuwenhuis made the same proposal at the following congress in 1893. Similar proposals were subsequently put forward regularly by French delegates, proposing to answer a war declaration with a general strike.

The resolution adopted by the 1896 congress declared that the working class demands:

> 1. The simultaneous abolition of standing armies and the establishment of a national citizen force.
>
> 2. The establishment of an international tribunal of arbitration whose decision shall be final.
>
> 3. The final decision on the question of war or peace to be vested directly in the people in cases where the governments refuse to accept the decision of the tribunal of arbitration.
>
> And it protests against the system of secret treaties.

In 1900 these demands were supplemented by other ones:

> 1. The different socialist parties should carefully instruct and organize the youth in the fight against militarism.
>
> 2. Socialist deputies in all countries should vote against military and naval expenditures, especially in cases of colonial aggression.
>
> 3. The permanent International Socialist Committee should organize in all countries a common and combined antimilitarist agitation and movement of protest.[5]

* * *

The Stuttgart Congress of 1907 was the scene of the most contentious discussion in the Second International on militarism and war. Most of the debate occurred in the congress's militarism commission, extending over five days and attended by hundreds of delegates.

Four resolutions were originally presented to the commission. The main one, put forward by August Bebel on behalf of the German Social Democratic Party (SPD), was largely a restatement of resolutions adopted at previous congresses, condemning capitalist militarism and presenting vague calls for international working-class action: "In case of war being imminent, the workers and their parliamentary representatives in the countries concerned shall be obligated to do everything possible to prevent the outbreak of war by resorting to whatever means they deem most effective, and in the event that it does break out nonetheless, to ensure that it ends quickly."

A second resolution, put forward by Jean Jaurès and Édouard Vaillant for the majority of the French delegation, called for energetic antimilitarist action "by means of the organized and combined efforts of the national and international socialist workers' organization. Such action in the countries concerned, and according to circumstances, should utilize all the energy and effort of the working class to prevent and stop the war by all means—including public parliamentary action, popular demonstrations, general strike, and insurrection."

A more extreme version of this perspective was presented in a resolution by Gustave Hervé, which stated: "Faced with diplomatic incidents from whatever side that threaten the peace of Europe, the Congress urges all citizens to respond to every war declaration—wherever it comes from—by a military strike and insurrection." The Hervé resolution also expressed opposition to all patriotism and to national defense.

The final resolution, put forward by Jules Guesde for the French minority, rejected any special antiwar measures, stating: "The Congress declares that the only campaign against militarism and for peace that is not utopian or a danger is a socialist campaign to organize the workers of the entire world to destroy capitalism."

A debate over these resolutions took place in the congress commission on war and international conflicts. A subcommission was then established to prepare a draft for the congress plenary. In this smaller body, Rosa Luxemburg submitted a series of amendments to Bebel's resolution prepared by her, V. I. Lenin, and Julius Martov. These amendments sharpened the Bebel resolution, spelling out the need not just for the working class to oppose these wars formally but also to take concrete action against them, and to do so in such a way as to advance the perspective of proletarian revolution.

The Luxemburg-Lenin-Martov amendments were incorporated into Bebel's draft, and the amended resolution was unanimously adopted by the commission and presented to the congress plenary, where it was also adopted without opposition.[6]

The final paragraph of the amended resolution was repeated verbatim in subsequent Second International resolutions: "In case war should break out notwithstanding, [socialists] shall be bound to intervene for its speedy termination, and to employ all their forces to utilize the economic and political crisis created by the war in order to rouse the masses of the people and thereby hasten the downfall of capitalist class rule."

* * *

While the Stuttgart resolution of 1907 was adopted unanimously, underlying disagreements remained. A month after the Stuttgart Congress, different perspectives were expressed at the annual congress of the German SPD, where the question of national defense was debated as well as the distinction between offensive and defensive wars.

This distinction was generally clear cut during some of the nineteenth-century national wars, in which it was possible to readily distinguish wars of conquest from those to defend national sovereignty. But such a distinction came to have less significance in the era of imperialist conflicts. During World War I, for example, the question of offensive versus defensive war was constantly used by Second International majority leaders to mask the war aims of their respective rulers and to obscure the imperialist character of the war.

The dispute at the 1907 SPD congress centered on remarks that right-wing Social Democrat Gustav Noske had made to the Reichstag in April 1907, stating that "it is damn well our duty and obligation to see to it that the German people are not shoved up against the wall by some other nations. If anyone should try to do that, we would of course defend ourselves with as much resolution" as the right-wing bourgeois parties.[7]

At the congress, Noske's remarks were strongly rejected by the party left wing, but they were defended by August Bebel, who stated that "we must defend the fatherland if it is attacked." Karl Kautsky answered Bebel, pointing out the uselessness of the offensive/defensive distinction in this case:

> Some day the German government might make the German proletarians believe they were being attacked; the French government might do the same with the French proletarians, and we would then have a war in which the French and German workingmen would follow their respective governments with equal enthusiasm and murder each other and cut each other's throats. That must be avoided, and it will be avoided if we do not adopt the criterion of the aggressive war, but that of proletarian interests which at the same time are international interests.[8]

The disagreements expressed at the SPD's 1907 congress remained unresolved, bursting forth openly with the outbreak of the First World War.

* * *

The Second International's Copenhagen Congress of 1910 occurred in the context of the arms buildup that characterized the years leading up to 1914. During this period Britain, Germany, and other powers were developing new weaponry while substantially increasing military spending.

At the congress, discussion on militarism and war focused on the questions of disarmament and arbitration of international disputes. Arguing in the militarism commission, Karl Radek pointed out the utopian nature of many disarmament demands. Most other commission members, however, disputed Radek's argument.

The congress also took up an amendment submitted by Vaillant and Keir Hardie: "Among the means to be used in order to prevent and hinder war, the Congress considers as particularly effective the general strike, especially in the industries that supply war with its implements (arms and ammunition, transport, etc.), as well as propaganda and popular action in their most active forms." It was decided to postpone discussion on this amendment to the next world congress, scheduled for the summer of 1914. That congress was among the first casualties of World War I.

The resolution ultimately adopted by the Copenhagen congress restated the conclusions of the Stuttgart resolution. However, there was little in the discussion to inspire confidence that the revolutionary perspective embodied in that resolution would be put into practice.

* * *

One thing the 1907 and 1910 debates clearly revealed was that illusions existed within the Second International on questions of war and peace, illustrated by Bebel's claim at the 1907 congress that "no one in the German ruling circles wants war." Similar illusions were shown in Copenhagen in 1910 regarding the ability of international agreements and treaties among imperialist powers to stop war. An example of such wishful thinking was Edouard Vaillant's statement during the 1910 debate that "[w]ars can be prevented for many generations." These illusions and the unclarity over the tasks of the working class in the fight against imperialist war would crystallize over the next four years.

Responding to illusions within the socialist movement on the question of peace and capitalist disarmament, Rosa Luxemburg addressed the issue in 1911, summarizing socialist tasks in the fight against militarism and war:

> To explain this to the masses, ruthlessly to scatter all illusions with regard to attempts made at peace on the part of the bourgeoisie and to declare the proletarian revolution as the first and only step toward world peace—that is the task of the social democrats with regard to all disarmament trickeries, whether they are invented in Petersburg, London or Berlin.[9]

In 1912, following the outbreak of the First Balkan War that foreshadowed the world conflict that would begin two years later, the Second International organized a special congress in Basel, Switzerland. That gathering adopted a resolution restating the conclusions of the Stuttgart resolution and asserting even more clearly the imperialist aims of the European capitalist powers. After the onset of World War I, the Basel Manifesto of 1912 would thus become a powerful tool to expose the Second International's majority leadership in 1914.

The Militarism and War Debate at the 1907 Stuttgart Congress

Proposed Resolutions

Hervé Resolution

Considering that national and governmental labels of the capitalists have little importance for the proletariat exploited by them, and that the class interests of the workers lie in the struggle against international capitalism without any diversion, the Congress repudiates bourgeois and governmental patriotism, which deceitfully affirms the existence of a community of interests among all the inhabitants of a country. The Congress affirms that the duty of socialists of every country is to fight to institute the collectivist or communist system and to defend it once they have succeeded in establishing it. Faced with diplomatic incidents from whatever side that threaten the peace of Europe, the Congress urges all citizens to respond to every war declaration—wherever it comes from—by a military strike and insurrection.

Guesde Resolution

Considering that militarism—as recognized by all international congresses—is the natural and necessary result of the capitalist system based on antagonistic class interests, which can disappear only when its cause disappears: the capitalist system;

Considering therefore that by having workers concentrate all efforts on eliminating militarism from present-day society, what is being done—whether intentionally or not—is a work of social conservation, diverting the working class from what should be its only concern: the seizure of political power, the expropriation of the capitalists, and the social appropriation of the means of production;

Considering, on the other hand, that the methods advocated by dupes or accomplices of antimilitarism (from desertion and military strikes up to insurrection) only complicate and make more difficult socialist propaganda and recruitment—delaying the moment when the proletariat will be sufficiently organized and strong to make the social revolution and put an end to militarism and all wars;

The Congress declares that the only campaign against militarism and for peace that is not utopian or a danger is a socialist campaign to organize the workers of the entire world to destroy capitalism. In the meantime, it is by the internationally organized reduction of military service; by the simultaneous refusal to grant all credits for war, navies, and colonies; and by the general arming of the people in place of standing armies—only through these measures can international conflicts be avoided to the extent possible. It is understood that as events arise that may lead to a conflict, the International [Socialist] Bureau should meet and do what is necessary.

Vaillant-Jaurès Resolution

I

The Congress confirms again the resolutions of previous international congresses:

1. For action against militarism and imperialism, which are nothing but the organized weapons of the state to maintain the working class under the economic and political yoke of the capitalist class.

2. To remind the working class of all countries that a government cannot threaten the independence of a foreign nation without attacking that nation, its working class, as well as the international working class. The threatened nation and its working class have the imperative duty of safeguarding their independence and autonomy against the attack, and the right to count on the assistance of the working class of all other

countries. To this effect, the antimilitarist and entirely defensive policy of the Socialist Party commands it to pursue military disarmament of the bourgeoisie and arming the working class, through the general arming of the people.

II

Confirming the decisions of previous international congresses and of the International Socialist Bureau:

The Congress considers international proletarian and socialist solidarity of all nations as its first duty.

The Congress issues a reminder that demonstrations are held every year on May First, whose necessary first consequence is the maintenance of international peace.

In face of the young Russian Revolution, of tsarism on the ropes and imperialist neighbors considering coming to its assistance, and of ceaseless capitalist and colonial piracy, the Congress urges the International Socialist Bureau and the Interparliamentary Conference,[10] with the consent of socialist parties of all countries, to make the necessary arrangements to bring together their delegates, in case of the threat of international conflict, to decide on measures to prevent and stop it.

The Congress urges that every possible effort be made to carry out these decisions by means of the organized and combined efforts of the national and international socialist workers' organization. Such action in the countries concerned, and according to circumstances, should utilize all the energy and effort of the working class to prevent and stop the war by all means—including public parliamentary action, popular demonstrations, general strike, and insurrection.

Bebel Resolution

Wars between states are as a rule the consequence of their competition on the world market, for every state is eager not only to preserve its markets but to acquire new ones, a policy in which the enslavement of foreign peoples and the confiscation of their lands plays a principal role.

The outbreak of wars is further promoted by national prejudices systematically cultivated in the interest of the ruling classes.

Wars are therefore essential to capitalism. They will not cease until the capitalist system has been done away with, or until the sacrifices in men and money required by the technical development of the military system and the rejection of the armaments race have become so great as to compel the nations to abandon this system.

The working class especially, from which the soldiers are chiefly recruited and which has to bear the greater part of the financial burdens, is by nature opposed to war, because war is irreconcilable with its aim: the creation of a new economic system founded on a socialist basis and realizing the solidarity of nations.

The Congress therefore considers it to be the duty of the working class, and especially its parliamentary representatives, to fight with all their might against military and naval armaments, not to grant any money for such purposes, pointing out at the same time the class character of bourgeois society and the real motives for maintaining national antagonisms.

The Congress considers that the democratic organization of national defense, by replacing the standing army with the armed people, will prove an effective means for making aggressive wars impossible, and for overcoming national antagonisms.

In case of war being imminent, the workers and their parliamentary representatives in the countries concerned shall be obligated to do everything possible to prevent the outbreak of war by resorting to whatever means they deem most effective, and in the event that it does break out nonetheless, to ensure that it ends quickly.

Commission Debate

August Bebel (Germany): We have debated and voted on the question of militarism and war at international congresses so often that, as I see it, simply reaffirming our previously adopted decisions would seem to be enough. [*"Very true!"*] But since the French comrades have requested that this question again be placed on the congress agenda—prompted mainly by Hervé's so-called antimilitarist agitation—we cannot avoid debating it once more. What Hervé says about militarism and patriotism in his book *Leur patrie* [Their country] is not new. Domela Nieuwenhuis already said it to all of us at previous congresses, [*"Very true!"*] and each congress rejected his views by a large majority. Today we maintain the same position.

Hervé says: "One's homeland is the homeland of the ruling classes. It is not a concern of the proletariat." A similar idea is expressed in the Communist Manifesto, which says: "The proletariat has no country." But students of Marx and Engels have declared that they no longer share the Manifesto's views on this. In addition, over the years Marx and Engels took positions that were very clear and in no way negative on the national question in Europe, including in Germany.

We do not fight against [the idea of] the homeland in and of itself, for it belongs to the proletariat far more than to the ruling classes. Rather, we combat the social relations that exist in this homeland to serve the interests of the ruling classes. [*"Very true!"*] Parliament too is an institution of the ruling classes, established to maintain their class rule. But we participate in parliament not only to fight ruling-class domination, but also to improve social conditions. We do not limit ourselves to being negative, but carry out positive work as well.

The cultural life and progress of a nation can develop only on the basis of complete freedom and independence, and through the medium of an established national language. For this reason, people everywhere suffering from foreign domination fight for national independence and freedom. We see this, for example, in Austria and in the struggle of the Poles to restore their national independence. As soon as Russia becomes a modern state, the nationalities question will arise there too.

Rosa Luxemburg (Poland): I don't think so!

Bebel (continues): I know that you have a different viewpoint, but I think you're wrong.[11]

Every nation under foreign domination fights first of all for its independence. Alsace-Lorraine fought against its separation from France, because for centuries its cultural development had progressed as a component of France and it enjoyed the conquests of the Great French Revolution.[12] Thus, its people possessed intimate cultural links to France without any disadvantages. Hervé thinks that it does not matter to the proletariat whether France belongs to Germany, or Germany to France—but that is absurd. [*Shouts of "That is not thinking at all!" Laughter*] I fear that if Hervé seriously explained this notion to his fellow compatriots, they would trample him underfoot. [*"Very true!"*]

In 1870, we saw what nationalist fever means in time of war. The masses perceived Napoleon [III] to be the culprit, although it was not he but Bismarck who provoked the declaration of war by falsifying the Ems Dispatch.[13] This became known only later. But in 1870 the nationalist fever targeted us as well, because we abstained on the vote to approve war credits. We held that both governments were to blame for the war, since the truth about the Ems Dispatch was not yet public knowledge.

I maintain that it is easy now to determine in any given case whether a war is defensive or whether it is offensive in character. While previously the causes leading to the catastrophe of war remained obscure even to trained and observant politicians, today that is no longer the case. War has ceased to be a matter of secret cabinet politics.

Let us also evaluate the practical meaning of antimilitarism as posed by Hervé. I don't know if Hervé's tactics are possible in France. I'm afraid, however, that in wartime we will have bad experiences there if we apply Hervé's methods of mass strike, desertion by the reservists and militia, and open insurrection. [*Agreement*] I must flatly state that for us these methods are not just impossible, but totally undiscussable.

The case of Karl Liebknecht shows how things stand today in Germany. Even though he clearly expressed his differences with Hervé in his book, and stated that Hervé's methods are unworkable, Liebknecht has been charged with high treason.[14] And I believe that the antimilitarist agitation Hervé is conducting may well be of dubious merit even from his own point of view. His activity is followed very closely by German military circles and by the German general staff. The prowar party, which is small here and still has no adherents in government circles, welcomes any sign of weakness among possible opponents. [*"Very true!"*]

No one in the German ruling circles wants war. This is in large part due to the existence of the socialist movement. Even Prince Bülow himself admitted to me that the governments know what would be at stake for the state and society in a great European war, and therefore would avoid it if possible.

For the reasons already stated, we also cannot vote for the Jaurès-Vaillant resolution. In its concluding sentence this resolution makes serious concessions to Hervéism. In addition, we are not obligated to make public statements about such things.

We are in agreement on the issue before us: the struggle against militarism and war. In the last forty years, we German socialists have fought against both militarism and war more consistently than in any other country. [*"Very true!"*] Jaurès is frequently held up, in contrast to us, as a model of patriotism.

Jean Jaurès (France): Exactly as you are to me in France!

Bebel (continues): Very true! In France, I am presented as a "great patriot" who is for every war, even if it's not a defensive one. In Germany, they sing quite a different tune.

During the Morocco crisis we did all we could both here and in France to prevent war.[15] As Social Democrats we realize that we cannot completely do without military weaponry. So long as the relations among states have not fundamentally changed, we allow for armaments but only for purely defensive purposes and on a broad and democratic basis in order to prevent misuse by the military. In Germany, therefore, we struggle with all our strength against the prevailing militarism, as expressed in the army, the navy, and any other form. Beyond that, however, we must not allow ourselves to be pressured into using methods of struggle that could gravely threaten the activity and, under certain circumstances, the very existence of the party.

I hope that after the conclusion of the general debate, the subcommission will succeed in coming to an agreement. [*Enthusiastic applause*]

Gustave Hervé (France): I was not aware that the general staff in Berlin is following with such satisfaction the progress of antimilitarist ideas in France. But I do know one thing for certain: French socialism and the French republic have been anxiously awaiting Bebel's speech—and it can only produce feelings of astonishment and sadness. [*Protests*]

Jules Guesde (France): I protest.

Hervé (continues): The same attitude left you in a minority at the Nancy Congress.[16]

What is the origin of the antimilitarist and antipatriotic campaign in France? It was during the most feverish days of the Russian Revolution [of 1905], when we heard threats that Prussian bayonets would invade Poland and be used against the Russian revolutionaries. We asked ourselves what the German Social Democracy would do to oppose such an outrageous act and feared that it might do nothing more than throw the moral weight of its three million votes into the scales. [*Laughter*]

The same question came up during the Morocco crisis, when the clouds of war gathered over Germany and France. Once again, we asked ourselves what German Social Democracy would do. Once again, its response carried only the moral weight of its three million votes.

Bebel has most obligingly informed me that, as a historical fact, homelands exist today in Europe. But I have learned still more interesting things from Bebel. At the Amsterdam Congress he told us: "Whether German monarchy or French republic: for us socialists it's all the same."[17] I say the same thing to you today. For the capitalists, every motherland represents the exploitation of the working majority by the bourgeois minority. The workers churn the butter for the rich man's table. Such a motherland is a harsh, evil stepmother indeed!

We aim to separate the capitalist wolves from their working-class prey by uniting the workers across national borders. Our class: that is our homeland.

Bebel draws a fine distinction between offensive and defensive war. Thus, when tiny Morocco is carved up, it is recognized to be an offensive war of unconcealed brutality. But should war break out between the great powers, the only-too-powerful capitalist press will unleash such a storm of nationalism that we will not have the strength to counteract it. Then it will be too late to make your fine distinction.

When did you learn of the falsification of the Ems Dispatch? Ten years after the murderous war. My antimilitarist agitation should act as a loud cry, a shout of warning to the German Social Democracy to do their duty to the International and make war impossible. My agitation in France had the greatest, most effective, and most outstanding success. [*Laughter*] I have been able to publicly explain my antimilitarist views in every city and village in France, confronting the bourgeoisie—and I have not been trampled on. Is that not a first-rate success?

At this year's French party congress in Nancy, the much-ridiculed Hervéists tipped the scale in favor of Jaurès and Vaillant and against Guesde on the question of militarism. [*Objection from Jaurès*] We thought that our splendidly successful agitation would set an example for you German socialists, which would spur you on. . . .

Bebel has left us no illusions as to whether or not the German Social Democracy will follow our example.

I do not at all deny the great achievements of Marx, Engels, Lassalle, Kautsky, Bebel, and also Eduard Bernstein—the only one today with some courage. But you have now become an electoral and accounting machine, a party of cash registers and parliamentary seats. [*Laughter*] You want to conquer the world with ballots. But I ask you: When the German soldiers are sent off to reestablish the throne of the Russian tsar, when Prussia and France attack the proletarians, what will you do? Please do not answer with metaphysics and dialectics, but openly and clearly—practically and tactically: What will you do?

I know that, in 1871, Bebel was imprisoned as a rebel. When Bismarck's government persecuted you, hundreds of you defied the German prisons.[18] You took risks in the face of Bismarck's iron laws because your political rights and electoral progress were being infringed upon. But today, when it would be a matter of preventing a clash that would cost the lives of hundreds of thousands of French and German workers, to judge from Bebel's speech, you are no longer able to take such risks.

Luxemburg: That is not true!

Hervé (continues): Naturally I'm not referring to you.[19] But we hear nothing about defying the law.

Bebel: You do not know that at all. We have endured ten times more prison terms than all the French antimilitarists put together!

Hervé (continues): On the contrary, the whole German Social Democracy has now become bourgeois. Today Bebel went over to the revisionists when he told us: "Proletarians of all countries, murder each other!" [*Loud commotion*] If you do not want us to carry on antimilitarist propaganda, then we will not have worked for peace, but for war.

Émile Vandervelde (Belgium): You are always working *pour le roi de Prusse!* [for the king of Prussia].[20] [*Laughter*]

Hervé (continues): Well, in questions of national conflicts, Belgium is not really a factor. [*Commotion*]

I was eager to get to know the German Social Democracy personally. For years I knew it only when I shrugged my shoulders at those quibbling, hairsplitting disputes over the interpretation of Karl Marx. Now I have seen the German proletarians here on the streets of Stuttgart.

My naive illusions are destroyed. It turns out that they are all good, satisfied, and well-fed solid citizens. [*Resounding laughter*]

We have morally disarmed the French general staff, since they know that war would mean a rebellion by the proletariat. But the blind obedience of you German Social Democrats to "Kaiser Bebel" is a deathlike discipline. Your approach makes war very possible. And if you march into war for your kaiser, without offering resistance, you will be marching against revolutionary communes, thrusting your bayonets into the breasts of French proletarians who are defending their barricades under the red flag of revolution. [*Commotion, laughter, and some applause*]

If German Social Democracy has nothing other than Bebel, I fear that our internationalism is only a deception of the proletariat.

Édouard Vaillant (France): . . . In the event of a war alert, we want the International Socialist Bureau to advise measures on our behalf to prevent the conflict. It is, however, important that this intervention be successful. The forces of the proletariat need to be prepared and deployed, as Lassalle wanted. What is possible in one place may not be possible elsewhere, but preparations can be made. That is why the International must determine the necessary means of action. In one case, parliamentary action may be sufficient. In other circumstances, it will be necessary to move toward more decisive action, combining popular agitation capable of preventing conflicts and wars. The facts themselves will give rise to the methods to be used. One may object that problems and inconveniences may arise in certain nations. The words in the resolution matter little. What we care about are deeds. In the French Empire, the necessary formulas have been found to say everything.

It is necessary that the International no longer be a large force whose weapons are latent, with its arms dangling helplessly, assisting in events. Rather, it must be a living force that knows how to push back our enemies, until the day comes when they can be annihilated. [*Applause*]

Jaurès: I come to defend the Vaillant resolution, whose formula was approved by the majority of the French Socialist Party. The French section wanted to mark the importance of this resolution by entrusting its defense to two men who were once divided but today are reconciled in the struggle.[21]

I also remain faithful to the same policy of action that I defended in Amsterdam. At that time, I asked socialists in parliament for their maximum effort in the interests of the proletariat. Today, I am asking the proletariat for its maximum action to prevent conflicts and fight war.

We reject Hervé's thesis because his methods of struggle are bad and are inappropriate to the requirements of time and place. According to Hervé, the homeland should be destroyed. We instead want to socialize the homeland for the benefit of the proletariat by putting the means of production under common ownership. [*Applause*] The nation is the treasure house of human genius and progress; destroying these precious reservoirs of human culture would harm the proletariat. [*"Very good!"*]

Our resolution has nothing to do with Hervéism. It did not accidentally pop up like the whim of some dreamer, but grew necessarily out of the big crises we experienced after the Fashoda Incident and the Morocco crisis. The proletariat must ask itself: Should we tolerate these crimes against humanity that are perpetrated for the benefit of a few capitalists? Should we not combat them through a great alliance of the powerful and organized working masses? Is that a dream? Is that a utopia?

Previously, national prejudices could make war unavoidable—as when Italy freed itself from Austria's domination or when Germany was only able to unify itself through blood and iron.[22] But now these national pretexts have disappeared. Thus, in the Morocco crisis, the first thought of the French and German proletarians was to unite. After Fashoda, the English trade unions came to a mighty peace demonstration in Paris, but only long after the danger of war had passed.[23] And they told us that the danger of proletarian fratricide had taken them by surprise. In the future will we also let ourselves be taken by surprise? No! Preventive measures must be taken now to unite the proletarian forces into an invincible army.

Some say that the struggle against war is futile since war is engendered inevitably by capitalism. But capitalism has exactly the same inherent tendency to increase exploitation without limit and to endlessly lengthen the workday. Yet still we fight for the eight-hour day, and with some success. [*"Very good!"*] . . .

In *Die Neue Zeit,* Kautsky called for direct action should German troops intervene in Russia to aid the tsar. Bebel repeated this statement from the rostrum of the Reichstag. If you could say it then, you can say it in every international conflict. [*"Very good!"*] German military intervention on the tsar's behalf against the Russian Social Democracy would certainly be the most acute, most extreme form imaginable of the class struggle.

Alarmed by the growth of the socialist movement, a government might attempt to create a foreign diversion rather than directly battle Social Democracy. If a war breaks out in this way between France and Germany, would we permit the French and German proletariat to murder one another on behalf of the capitalists and for their benefit without Social Democracy attempting to exert the greatest effort to stop it? [*"Very good!"*] If we were not to make the attempt, we would all be dishonored. [*Stormy applause*]

Bebel has described for us the dangers of antimilitarist agitation in Germany. We definitely do not want to risk the destruction of the strongest branch of international socialism. But I think you are exaggerating. You have already gone through the test of the Anti-Socialist Laws, when a heavier hand came down upon you than that of some Prussian minister.[24] The government can make an individual feel the severity of the law, but it cannot crush the strength of three million. . . .

If a conflict between France and Germany were to break out, chauvinist brutality would be unleashed indiscriminately against all of us—even against the cleverest and most careful. [*Applause*] We should therefore be open enough to say that, although we recognize the inviolability of every country and will not give up any country to the exploitation and oppression of another, we will not allow the international proletariat to be massacred. For thirty years, the German party program has called for resolving international conflicts through arbitration courts. Given the increasing power of Social Democracy, the capitalist class has now made this slogan of international socialism one of their own demands. . . .

We can put every government in a real predicament if we demand that they submit to an international court of arbitration in the event of an international conflict. If they refuse, we can denounce them as the biggest enemy of world peace. [*"Very good!"*]

Comrades! The whole capitalist world is watching this congress. The strength of international socialism and its growth, as revealed by this congress, surprises them. The immeasurable and inexhaustible proletarian force represented by the 880 delegates here also surprises them. We, who have so proudly proclaimed the bankruptcy of the bourgeoisie, must never permit it to speak of a bankruptcy of the International on this vital question. [*Stormy, prolonged, and repeated applause*]

Georg von Vollmar (Germany) . . . Far be it from me to consider Citizen Hervé as the spokesperson for the French comrades, to hold them responsible for everything he says. I have no intention of getting into the internal affairs preoccupying our comrades in France. But I want to call your attention to the danger of being too condescending to Citizen Hervé. Indeed, when Jaurès and Vaillant deny speaking the language that Hervé himself considers brutal, they nevertheless reach the same conclusions. With good reason, Hervé could triumphantly proclaim that he was allied with Jaurès and Vaillant in getting the resolution approved at Nancy.

I say this because Jaurès gave us the good advice to not exaggerate Hervé's importance. It seems to me that our French comrades themselves do not take Hervé's agitation too seriously. But it would be better for them to reject all his ideas, rather than rejecting them halfway and accepting the essence of his conclusions. . . .

Moving on from Hervé. I will now take up the Jaurès-Vaillant resolution. On this question I agree with many of the points Bebel made. . . .

It is not true that "international" means "antinational." It is not true that we have no homeland. And I use the word "homeland" without adding some hairsplitting elucidation of the concept. I know why socialism must be international, but my love for humanity can never prevent me from being a good German, just as it cannot prevent others from being good citizens of France or Italy. We recognize the common cultural interests of all peoples and condemn and fight against the incitement of nationalist hatreds. But we must also reject utopian chatter about the end of nations and their melting away into an amorphous porridge of peoples.

Jaurès: So who wants that?

Vollmar (continues): Comrade Jaurès, I know that you and Vaillant have said wonderful things about the need for national independence. But you are not alone in this room. As long as Citizen Hervé is in your party, you cannot simply shrug your shoulders and refuse to take responsibility for him.

We have good reason to laugh at the caricature of patriotism and national sentiment made by our adversaries. But at the same time, we do not want to give them the opportunity to present us in a disfigured way as the image of internationalism, to allow the ruling classes to wrap their egoism in the national mantle, and thus to awaken feelings of the whole nation against us.

Wilhelm Liebknecht once said: "The bloodthirsty beast will be brought down by the spirit of socialism, by propaganda, by education, and by achieving influence both in parliament and in public opinion—but not by childish conspiracies in the barracks."[25] The overwhelming majority of the German party has always supported this viewpoint. I would say the same thing about the other methods of struggle that are specified in the Jaurès-Vaillant resolution. . . .

As for Jaurès's reference to a statement by Kautsky, no one will fail to see the difference between an individual statement and the binding declaration of a whole party. Naturally, I will not take up here Karl Liebknecht's statement concerning antimilitarist agitation, because his case is now before the Supreme Court. But we do not argue against the methods outlined in the Jaurès-Vaillant resolution simply out of prudence.

More importantly, we see the resolution as absurd on the basis of principle. [*Objection by a number of French delegates, especially Hervé*] We believe it misconstrues the essence of socialist politics. Instead of comprehending social reality in its essence and context, only its outward appearance is considered. It is just as foolish to believe that the world can be rid of war through a strike against militarism, or something similar, as it is to think that you could do away with capitalism overnight by means of a general strike. To choose such tactics would be a step away from the correct road. . . .

You can be sure that we German Social Democrats are as well acquainted with the whole misery of war as are comrades in all other countries. And we are just as prepared as they to use all possible means to put a stop to the incitement of nationalist hatred and to use our growing influence on the ruling powers and on public opinion to prevent war. We are not going to insist on the wording of Bebel's resolution, and we are quite willing to come to an agreement. But we urgently request that you not tie us to certain methods of struggle. This would take away our right to freely determine our own policies and imperil the basis of our existence. [*German delegates: "Bravo!"*]

Chairperson Albert Südekum announces that he has received the following note from Comrade Karl Liebknecht:

I am not a member of the commission and therefore cannot speak here. I would therefore ask you to bring the following to the body's attention:

On Tuesday afternoon, Comrade Vollmar on two different occasions pulled me into the debate. He first quoted a statement made long ago by my father on barracks agitation, and he then asserted that the last three German party congresses had rejected proposals to initiate propaganda inside the barracks as dangerous childishness. This statement relates to proposals I myself made that were rejected, which had been aimed at encouraging specialized antimilitarist propaganda as a special branch of overall party activity. After this attack on my antimilitarist efforts, Comrade Vollmar added that in view of the pending trial against me, he did not want to deal with my pamphlet [*Militarism and Antimilitarism*].

I emphatically declare that I regret any such considerations and absolutely reject them. Rather, I state that the class-justice charges being brought against me by the capitalist class should serve to reinforce and intensify the antimilitarist attitude of the congress.

Émile Vandervelde (Belgium): . . . Hervé, by throwing his internationalist firebombs, has rendered a great service to the French proletariat, which they were trying to drag into patriotism. But his methods are inadmissible. He wants disarmament by everyone. Granted, it is difficult to distinguish between defensive and offensive wars.

Take the Transvaal and Japan. In the event of war, socialists must agree on which side their interests lie. With regard to the Transvaal War, our British socialist comrades have protested against it. Similarly, in Japan's war, who was it that protested against tsarism? The Russian revolutionaries.[26] It is thus easy to determine which side is taken by the International.

I come to the Guesde resolution. I agree with him on the principle of self-defense, but I do not accept that antimilitarism is a diversion. Three years ago Guesde—inflexible sentry that he is—told the reformists that they were compromising socialist doctrine and action. He had only sarcasm for our socialist cooperatives that wanted to make socialism with bread. However, his friends imitated the Belgian cooperatives to the north. Certainly Guesde's inflexibility on principles was useful, but it should not degenerate into dogmatism. Beware of satisfying the petty bourgeoisie and those afraid of revolutionary action by fighting cooperatives, by fighting anti-alcoholism, by fighting antimilitarism.

As we understand it, socialism is nothing other than a synthesis of this triple effort, which all fit together, stemming from economic antagonisms. But it is not a diversion to take a position against militarism, rather than waiting for the day after the revolution.

In France, I would not have hesitated to vote for the Vaillant resolution. But what about here at the international congress? The German Social Democrats have raised some objections. It is not essential to list the means to employ on this question. The important thing is for the International to affirm its unanimity to stop war. There should be no division between French and German socialists on the obligation to prevent war by all means.

We want a strong resolution, but we also want to reach agreement. If we do not succeed, that is, if the French comrades declare themselves for the general strike and the German comrades against, then it will be an impossible situation for an international congress. The German delegates should think about that.

I am an old friend of the German comrades and have been their comrade in arms for twenty years. I have learned a great deal from them, and I owe them very much. I ask you German comrades: Are you not willing to learn something this time from the experience of other countries? The majority of the congress thinks that it would not be good if the French comrades threw themselves into antimilitarist agitation, while the German comrades held themselves entirely aloof. . . .

Victor Adler (Austria): The Austrian comrades are completely in agreement with Vandervelde's speech, whose content and tone I support. But I must begin by polemicizing with Vandervelde. He spoke of the usefulness of Hervé's firebombs as a counterweight to chauvinism. I don't normally get involved in questions foreign to my country, but I nevertheless observe that Guesde and Vaillant protested against revanchist policy during the 1880s and '90s, which at that time was more dangerous than today.[27]

Excesses similar to Hervé's are not lacking in all countries. If Vandervelde wants to have such people and if Belgium needs them, we are happy to export ours, as we have little need of them. The struggle is not between Hervé and us, but between the French and German methods of expressing socialism's ideas on militarism. For us, Hervé is a type of Baroness of Suttner.[28] [*Laughter*]

Socialist antimilitarism arises from our understanding of the political and economic process, and then from international solidarity of the proletariat itself. It is not limited to a specific action at a given moment, but rather constitutes an integral part of the great proletarian movement.

We do not need to wait for the hour of a war declaration in order to work against war. All of our party's actions, all of our work to stop war—that is genuine antimilitarist action. We do not need special slogans. Perhaps our words are not drastic enough. On this point we cannot compete with our comrades from other countries. But we say to you that our way of acting in Austria, as in Germany, is not simply socialist and internationalist, but also antimilitarist and directed against war. . . .

We wish to declare categorically in the resolution that the congress views as one of its greatest tasks making the proletariat conscious that war is an attack on its very existence and that war should be fought using all means. We want our weapons of defense to be as strong as possible, and if the Germans say that this resolution is a weapon for later, we easily believe them.

But I do not want to accept Vollmar's views without reservation. In this resolution we cannot bind ourselves to either a positive or a negative formula. That is the position that we in Austria have taken toward the general strike. On the other hand, we have declared that we do not reject any means. Our duty is to concentrate all the proletariat's forces that are necessary at a specific moment in a given country.

We lean to voting for the Bebel resolution, because everything I've said is there. . . .

Luxemburg: I have asked for the floor in order to remind you, on behalf of the Russian and Polish Social Democratic delegations, that at this point on the agenda we should all consider the great Russian Revolution. At the opening of the congress when Vandervelde, with characteristic eloquence, duly expressed our gratitude to its martyrs, we all rendered homage to the victims, the fighters. But after hearing many speeches, and especially Vollmar's, it occurred to me that were the bloody ghosts of the revolutionaries here, they would say: "We give you back your homage, but learn from us!" And it would be a betrayal of the revolution for you not to do so.

The last congress, in 1904 at Amsterdam, discussed the mass strikes and decided that we were too immature and unprepared for them.[29] But materialist dialectics, so convincingly invoked by Victor Adler, has suddenly accomplished what we declared to be impossible. I must now speak against Vollmar, and unfortunately against Bebel too. They say we are not in a position to do more than we have done up to now. The Russian Revolution, however, did not merely result from the Russo-Japanese War; it also served to put an end to it. Otherwise, tsarism would surely have continued the war. The dialectics of history does not mean that we wait with arms folded until it bears us ripe fruit.

I am a convinced adherent of Marxism, and for this very reason I consider it very dangerous to mold the Marxist method into a rigid fatalistic form. This only calls forth, in return, such excesses as Hervéism. Hervé is an *enfant*, although an *enfant terrible* to be sure. [*Laughter*]

Vollmar said of Kautsky that he spoke only in his own name. This is even more true of Vollmar. The fact is that most German party members have disavowed Vollmar's point of view. This happened at the Jena party congress, where a resolution was adopted almost unanimously that showed the German party to be a revolutionary party that has learned from history. In this resolution the party declared that the general strike, which it had denounced for years as anarchistic, was a method of struggle that could be applied under certain circumstances.[30] It was not the spirit of Domela Nieuwenhuis, but the red ghost of the Russian Revolution that hovered over the deliberations at Jena. Of course, we had in mind then a mass strike for suffrage rather than against the war. While we cannot swear to carry out a mass strike if we are deprived of suffrage, neither can we swear that it is only for suffrage that we will carry out such a strike.

In view of the speech by Vollmar—and also to some extent the one by Bebel—we consider it necessary to sharpen Bebel's resolution. We have drafted an amendment to be submitted later. In it we go further, to a certain degree, than Comrades Jaurès and Vaillant. Our amendment contends that, in case of war, our agitation should aim at not merely ending the war, but also utilizing it to hasten the overthrow of class rule in general. [*Applause*]

Russell Smart (Britain): The Hervé resolution is not at all suitable for Britain, because no British government is capable of conducting a war without the consent of the overwhelming majority of the working class. But if the public were whipped up into a nationalist frenzy, a military strike would then be pure lunacy. In the struggle against war, therefore, under no circumstances can the British Social Democracy go beyond peaceful activity in Parliament, at conferences, and in the streets.

The British section cannot attach any practical importance to the remarks by Jaurès. If a new war breaks out, British socialists would act exactly like they did during the Transvaal War, refusing to do anything violent that would make them look ridiculous. On the other hand, the German and French resolutions are equally unacceptable to us in their present forms, because they call for a general arming of the population. A general arming of the population is progressive when the people are already militarized. In Britain that would be a step backwards, because our bourgeoisie—which is smarter than those on the continent—is currently propagandizing among our workers in favor of general service.

British soldiers do not shoot at the people. That was clearly shown during the labor unrest in Belfast where unfortunately there were deaths, but two were not on the side of the strikers.[31] These figures prove that the British soldiers shoot into the air, not at the people. British freedom allows us to discuss this question without the least danger. Therefore we must alter the resolutions to adjust them to British conditions through an amendment against the demand for arming the entire people. That is the position of the Independent Labour Party. [*Applause*]

Bebel: . . . Things were presented in this debate as if there were big differences among us, as if the Germans refused to fight militarism and did not understand how to carry out their duty to the International. Comrades, there is not a single German socialist that had this idea.

When we took up the militarism question at previous international congresses, we were always on the side of the big majority of the International, and we have not changed our conception. Our French comrades, on the contrary, have changed their position, thereby creating division. [*Protests from the French seats*] We know better than you how to interpret the final sentence of the Nancy resolution.[32] We do not want to put ourselves in difficulties for no reason, paralyzing the forces of our movement.

This morning Adler sketched very clearly the dialectical development of militarism. If I am not mistaken about the external forms, it would be better to go further than he did and state that militarism has reached a point in its development in which we can say that the first time it tries to carry things out, it will break its neck. Our resolutions would not cause the slightest harm to militarism had not its own development over the last forty years undermined the basis of its very existence. . . .

A Social Democrat might say that in a certain sense a great European war would advance our cause more than decades of agitation have, and so we should hope for it. But we do not wish for such a dreadful means of reaching our goal. However, if those who have the greatest stake in maintaining bourgeois society cannot perceive that such a war would uproot it, then we cannot object. I then say: "Just keep right at it, we shall be your heirs." [*Enthusiastic applause; laughter from the Hervéists*] Had the ruling class not known this, we would long ago have seen a European-wide war. Only the fear of Social Democracy has prevented it thus far. [*"Very true!"*] If such a war does break out, then much more will be at stake than mere trifles such as insurrection and mass strike. Then the entire civilized world will change, from the ground up. If we understand this, we do not need to argue over the methods of struggle to be used at such a moment.

The German resolution clearly and unequivocally states that we combat militarism with all the means that we deem effective. We cannot yet determine our tactics in advance; we cannot yet impose them on our enemy.

Earthshaking events can transform our minority into a majority. Never before in the history of the civilized world has a movement embraced the masses as profoundly as does the socialist movement. Never before has a movement given the despised masses such an insight into the nature of our society. Never have there been so many who knew what they wanted from the state and society. Let us keep our eyes open and our heads clear, so that we are prepared for the moment when it comes. [*Enthusiastic, prolonged applause*] . . .

Adopted Resolution

The Congress reaffirms the resolutions passed by previous international congresses against militarism and imperialism, and it again declares that the fight against militarism cannot be separated from the socialist class struggle as a whole.

Wars between capitalist states are as a rule the consequence of their competition in the world market, for every state is eager not only to preserve its markets but also to conquer new ones, principally by the subjugation of foreign nations and the confiscation of their lands. These wars are further engendered by the unceasing and ever-increasing armaments of militarism, which is one of the principal instruments for maintaining bourgeois class rule and for subjugating the working classes politically and economically.

The outbreak of wars is further promoted by the national prejudices systematically cultivated in the interest of the ruling classes in order to divert the masses of the proletariat from their class duties and international solidarity.

Wars are therefore essential to capitalism; they will not cease until the capitalist system has been done away with, or until the sacrifices in men and money required by the technical development of the military system and the rejection of the armaments race have become so great as to compel the nations to abandon this system.

The working class especially, from which the soldiers are chiefly recruited, and which has to bear the greater part of the financial burdens, is by nature opposed to war, because war is irreconcilable with its aim: the creation of a new economic system founded on a socialist basis and realizing the solidarity of nations.

The Congress therefore considers it to be the duty of the working class, and especially of its parliamentary representatives, to fight with all their might against military and naval armaments, not to grant any money for such purposes, pointing out at the same time the class character of bourgeois society and the real motives for maintaining national antagonisms, and further, to imbue working-class youth with the socialist spirit of universal brotherhood and developing their class consciousness.

The Congress considers that the democratic organization of national defense, by replacing the standing army with the armed people, will prove an effective means for making aggressive wars impossible, and for overcoming national antagonisms.

The International cannot lay down rigid formulas for action by the working class against militarism, as this action must of necessity differ according to the time and conditions of the various national parties. But it is the duty of the International to intensify and coordinate, as much as possible, the efforts of the working class against militarism and war.

In fact, since the Brussels Congress [of 1891], the proletariat in its untiring fight against militarism, by refusing to grant the expenses for military and naval armaments, by democratizing the army, has had recourse, with increasing vigor and success, to the most varied methods of action in order to prevent the outbreak of wars, or to end them, or to make use of the social convulsions caused by war for the emancipation of the working class: as for instance the understanding arrived at between the British and French trade unions after the Fashoda crisis, which served to assure peace and to reestablish friendly relations between Britain and France; the action of the socialist parties in the German and French parliaments during the Morocco crisis: the public demonstrations organized for the same purpose by the French and German socialists; the common action of the Austrian and Italian socialists who met at Trieste in order to ward off a conflict between the two states;[33] further, the vigorous intervention of the socialist workers of Sweden in order to prevent an attack against Norway;[34] and lastly, the heroic sacrifices and fights of the masses of socialist workers and peasants of Russia and Poland rising against the war provoked by the government of the tsar, in order to put an end to it and to make use of the crisis for the emancipation of their country and of the working class.[35] All these efforts show the growing power of the proletariat and its increasing desire to maintain peace by its energetic intervention.

The action of the working classes will be the more successful, the more the mind of the people has been prepared by an unceasing propaganda, and the more the labor parties of the different countries have been spurred on and coordinated by the International.

The Congress further expresses its conviction that under the pressure exerted by the proletariat, the practice of honest arbitration in all disputes will replace the futile attempts of the bourgeois governments, and that in this way the people will be assured of the benefits of universal disarmament, which will allow the enormous resources of energy and money, wasted by armaments and wars, to be applied to the progress of civilization.

In case of war being imminent, the working class and its parliamentary representatives in the countries concerned shall be bound, with the assistance of the International Socialist Bureau, to do all they can to prevent the outbreak of war, using for this purpose the means that appear to them the most effective and which must naturally vary according to the acuteness of the class struggle and to the general political conditions.

In case war should break out notwithstanding, they shall be bound to intervene for its speedy termination and to employ all their forces to utilize the economic and political crisis created by the war in order to rouse the masses of the people and thereby hasten the downfall of capitalist class rule.

The Militarism and War Debate at the 1910 Copenhagen Congress

Proposed Resolutions

Social Democratic Party of Germany Report

The question of disarmament was dealt with thoroughly by the German Reichstag during the winter of 1908–1909. The Social Democratic Group in the Reichstag had taken advantage of the statements by the British prime minister, Mr. Asquith, made in the House of Commons on March 16, 1909, concerning an agreement intended to reduce expenditures on naval armaments. The representative of the German foreign ministry had made only equivocal statements about this affair, and it was at this point that our fraction presented to the Reichstag a resolution "urging the Chancellor of the Empire, with regard to the resolutions of the The Hague conferences of 1899 and 1907—approved by the German government—to take steps as soon as possible to prepare an international agreement of the powers for the mutual limitation of naval armaments and to reach accord on renouncing the right of seizure in naval warfare."

This resolution was discussed in the Reichstag on March 29, 1909. The speaker of the Social Democratic Group referred above all to the demonstrations for peace by British workers. He declared that the Social Democratic Group, as far as disarmament is concerned, completely agrees with the representatives of the Labour Party in the British House of Commons. An understanding would surely be possible if Germany consented to a limitation of armaments and if Britain agreed to the abolition of the right of seizure in naval warfare. The Chancellor, Prince von Bülow, replied that it had not yet been possible to find a formula that could be used for an international understanding on the question of disarmament. He then claimed that Germany would never do more than exercise its natural right: to refuse any discussion with foreigners on the internal affairs of Germany. It goes without saying that any international agreement would be impossible were such a principle adhered to. This absurd sentence by Prince von Bülow nevertheless earned him the applause of all bourgeois parties, including the Liberals, who are part of the International League for Peace! Only one Liberal politician voted with the Social Democrats for the socialist motion asking to make the necessary preparations to begin negotiations aimed at limiting naval armaments.

It is certainly characteristic that in recent years the left Liberals, despite their tradition in previous decades, have voted for all military and naval funding requests by the government. Social Democracy is alone in Germany in the fight against militarism and naval buildups. The increase in the number of affiliates and subscribers of the Social Democratic Party, and the 3,250,000 socialist voters, is the best guarantee for maintaining peace in Germany. The ruling classes feared above all that the Social Democracy would profit from a war, as Prince von Bülow said in the Reichstag on December 5, 1904:

"The deputy Mr. Bebel then expressed the opinion that Social Democracy would first bear the fruits of a great European war. This conception seems correct to me, and it is one more reason for the governments of all countries to continue, as I believe they will do, their present peaceful policy, which is a calm and considered policy. . . ."

Independent Labour Party (Britain) Resolution

1. The Copenhagen International Congress reaffirms its previous resolutions, which state:

That the workers of all countries have neither disagreed nor differed with each other in a manner that could provoke war; that modern wars are waged solely in the interest and for the benefit of the ruling classes. Further, considering the appalling wastage of national and international resources now being made in preparation for war between European nations, the Congress emphatically declares that the time has come for concerted international action by the working people of all countries, to be defined by the Congress, leaving it to each nation to choose the best methods to put this resolution into practice.

2. The Independent Labour Party (ILP) recommends that the Congress consider the advisability of authorizing the International Bureau to organize a vigorous antiwar campaign, aimed at bringing about concerted action by the working class in the event of a threatened or decided-upon war between European nations, as well as to advocate the establishment of an international federation of European and constitutional countries in general, and to insist on the need to maintain armies and navies not as national forces, but as guardians of world peace.

Social Democratic Federation (Britain) Resolution

While recognizing that war is the necessary consequence of the antagonism of interests produced by the system of capitalist competition, the Congress nevertheless observes with deep apprehension the immense and rapid development of armaments and war preparations in all capitalist countries. It also notes that these armaments and other circumstances have the consequence of increasing the dangers that threaten world peace.

In view of these facts, the Congress reaffirms the resolutions of previous international socialist congresses concerning the action of Social Democracy against militarism, war, and imperialism, and it calls on socialists and workers of all countries to energetically pursue their campaign against aggressive imperialism, militarism, and armaments.

In opposition to imperialism and to defend the autonomy of all nationalities, the workers of every country should forcefully undertake agitation aimed at abolishing all standing armies and creating an armed nation. The workers must oppose all expenditure on armaments that are not absolutely necessary for national defense. They must demand the abolition of secret diplomacy, the publication of all existing treaties, and the submission of all draft treaties or agreements to a popular referendum. They must seize all opportunities that present themselves to encourage and strengthen feelings of solidarity among the peoples and to force the governments to refer all their disputes to tribunals of peaceful arbitration.

The Congress, moreover, mandates the International Bureau to take the necessary measures to convene a conference between the representatives of the workers' movement in the countries that find themselves threatened by the danger of war. That conference would have to decide what measures should be taken on both sides to best prevent war and avoid all aggressive acts that could serve as a pretext to start hostilities.

Italian SP Resolution

The Congress is of the opinion that, without prejudice toward other forms of propaganda and antimilitarist action accepted by the party, the policy that can best succeed in the shortest number of years is that of calling for a conference of European states with the aim of reducing by 50 percent, for the time being, the military forces under arms in all states, and also to suspend all subsequent increases in armaments.

To make this work effective, it is necessary that the various socialist parliamentary groups, without neglecting to attract allies, at the same time invite the governments to take the initiative in the aforementioned conference. They will repeat this invitation each year as often as possible, and for the next several years, and they will present the invitation in the same terms, especially on the occasion of the discussion of military budgets, foreign affairs budgets, and those related to army expansion. They will not be discouraged by the successive rejections of their proposal, and they should be happy enough to see a gradual increase in the support for their views within public opinion.

In order for this work to be accomplished with the necessary continuity and frequency, as well as carried out in the same way and at the same time in the various countries, the Congress is of the opinion that it is necessary to constitute in Berlin—the main center of European militarism—a secretariat having the exclusive responsibility for inviting the socialist groups to collaborate in the aforementioned work, as the opportunity arises in the various parliaments, and of reporting each group's actions to the daily press in all other countries.

French SP Resolution

Affirming once again that war can end only with the elimination of the capitalist order, the Congress declares that the Workers' International constitutes for the time being the best organ for the preservation of peace.

It has already carried out and will carry out for this purpose action that is all the more energetic and effective as it itself grows in strength and cohesion, and will be able in a more continuous and firm manner to translate into action the resolutions of the Stuttgart Congress and other of its congresses, especially in the case of the threat of armed conflicts between nations.

But it is precisely because the Workers' International is the best organ for the preservation of peace that it cannot ignore attempts made even outside itself to guarantee this same peace.

Without illusions as to the extent of the results that can be achieved in this way at the present time, but convinced that overall progress is being made out of the daily progress that is constantly achieved, the International will therefore act to compel governments to take seriously the increasing number of attempts to settle conflicts between nations amicably, and to ensure the most regular and generalized functioning possible of the arbitration courts that the capitalist bourgeoisie has been forced to set up, in large part, due to growing pressure from socialist opinion.

It will act in the same way to promote, in all countries, the development of a peaceful education, to be given by teachers to children and young people, in order to prepare generations for whom all militaristic and chauvinistic prejudices will be eliminated, and who will embrace in common sympathy all the members of the great human family.

In the same spirit again, it will make unceasing efforts to pursue the simultaneous disarmament of nations and the replacement of standing armies—instruments of invasion and conquest—by national militias, simple defensive forces.

Commission Debate

Édouard Vaillant (France): The abolition of war will first and foremost allow socialism to develop, but one cannot assume this will happen peacefully on its own. While recognizing that the International is an association to maintain peace, we should not disregard its efforts toward that end, even if they are brought about outside the socialist movement. The proletariat must prepare itself for every eventuality of a militaristic outbreak, as the bourgeois parties will not hesitate to resort to war if necessary to counteract the socialist thrust. . . .

Keir Hardie (Britain): . . . The strength of the workers is strong enough to prevent war. To be more certain of the result, this idea should be developed within the unions. The day war is declared, all workers should stop work.

Bruce Glasier (Britain): . . . It has been said that capitalism is the cause of war. That is wrong. War existed long before capitalism. Bestial behavior is the cause of war among men, and this has been the case since the beginning of human existence. If we consider capitalism as the only cause of war, the struggle against war will never be possible. Let us organize a large propaganda effort for passive resistance, and in this way we could reach an agreement among the united states of Europe. . . . A manifesto drafted in this sense was already put out by the International Workingmen's Association during the Franco-Prussian War.[36] We hope that something similar can be successfully accomplished today.

Karl Radek (Poland): The resolutions should be combined, but they're contradictory. Two different points of view are presented.

The demand has been raised for elimination of the fleets. This viewpoint, accepted by the Social Democratic fraction in the German Reichstag, is utopian and cannot possibly be supported with socialist arguments. Social Democrats should not demand such a transformation, because even if it were to be adopted, it would not be applied. Elimination of the navy would not be possible unless an international executive power existed capable of counterbalancing the opposing interests. But such a power does not exist, and we will not be able to institute it either. Such demands are therefore not possible. We can only raise our ideas.

The second point of view concerns naval limitations on Germany and Britain. The German government has not the slightest intention of going down this road. But it's nevertheless possible that, as a result of financial difficulties, the two governments will decide on reciprocal limits. The masses would have to be told that these measures relate purely to naval questions, since a limitation on fleets could lead to an increase in land armies. We cannot be satisfied with demanding either limitations or elimination of the British and German navies: we must also address ourselves to Russia. Note once more that the German and British press have already dealt with the need to have a naval presence in the seas of the East.

The stance taken by *Vorwärts* and the attitude of the Reichstag fraction are anti–social democratic. It is the counterpart of the position of Hyndman, who calls for new armaments.[37]

Georg Ledebour (Germany): . . . I will respond to the reproaches of Comrade Radek. If he is right, the attitude taken by the Social Democratic fraction in the Reichstag and *Vorwärts* is in contradiction to socialist principles. Radek has polemicized with *Vorwärts*. I don't take any responsibility for what's written in *Vorwärts*. But the stance taken by the German Reichstag fraction and *Vorwärts* has also been taken twice by the British comrades in the House of Commons. As things currently stand, we cannot always put forward purely socialist motions in parliament. Why is the proposal of the British comrades for reduction of the navy contrary to our principles? Why can't Social Democrats present proposals for disarmament?

We cannot, however, leave it to parliament to carry out these proposals for the future state. Radek seems not to be aware of the substance of the resolution and not to have read the justification for it.

Radek: I'm very well aware of the events, and I attacked the Reichstag fraction in the pages of the *Leipziger Volkszeitung*.[38]

Ledebour (continues): We have linked two questions: limitation on naval armaments and suppression of the right of seizure [at sea]. After we put forward this resolution, the German government felt compelled to declare that owing to the increase in British warships, it was obliged to reserve even more money for new naval construction. On that occasion we were able to again demonstrate the lies of Bülow and Tirpitz.

The bourgeois press will not be able to deny that socialists of all countries are united against war and that we are at the head of the movement. Our proposal had fruitful results. In the Reichstag only a single Liberal voted with the socialists, but little by little the bourgeoisie rallied to the idea of an agreement for naval limitations, without however acknowledging that this idea had been put forward by the Social Democrats.

In the British Parliament a large part of the bourgeoisie voted with the Labour Party. Without making purely socialist proposals—which was impossible in this matter—we have thereby fought the capitalist state. The question matures, and the idea is gaining ground.

A. M. Dessin (Britain, Social Democratic Federation): . . . Bruce Glasier believes that wars are not all due to capitalism, but arise from economic causes. If you dispute that, you are not a socialist. Modern wars are due above all to economic causes, therefore to capitalism. So if we do away with capitalism, we will eliminate war.

Vaillant (France): In Stuttgart we declared that we agreed on principles. Today we take up the means. Our resolution lays them out. Wars can be prevented for many generations. That is the aim of our proposals. Lebedour spoke of the value of the actions by German Social Democrats and British socialists—all the work they did to obtain disarmament.

The greatest danger at the present time is the lack of understanding between Germany and Britain. However, a war could set us back for many years. It is no longer a question of theoretical discussions, but of stopping war. There are things that can be done in present-day society. We want arbitration, but arbitration does not come on its own. Is it not the result of socialist action?

But there is another point of view: if we have been able to bring this to parliaments, it is the result of action outside parliaments. In Stuttgart, we declared ourselves against war. Now it is necessary to pass over to action, to propaganda. Keir Hardie said in his resolution that in case of war, all workers should refuse to work. In Stuttgart, we decided to employ all means against war. The general strike and insurrection are extreme means, but they should be employed if necessary.

Ledebour: . . . The resolution says that arbitration courts should be permanent institutions. Until now, arbitration has been optional. We call for arbitration courts that are obligatory in all cases. In this we differ with all the bourgeois parties. There are quite a few individuals of the bourgeoisie who would like to see this reform, but no party has yet taken it up. The constant renewal of such proposals have gone in the direction of general disarmament, or at least the limitation of naval armaments and the abolition of the right of naval seizure.

In Germany it's said that if a war breaks out, our ships will be beaten by the British navy. For this reason, we must have a navy to defend our merchant shipping. All this is simply a pretext, however, because the navy is unable to save merchant ships from piracy. I remind you simply of the history of the *Alabama*.[39] We seek precisely to stop such pillaging. We want merchant ships to be able to go in peace without having to fear pillaging. In this way, the argument about needing a fleet to protect merchant ships is invalid. . . .

Oddino Morgari (Italy): The resolution presented by the majority is a good socialist resolution. I support it, but it lacks effectiveness. What it highlights as the most serious threat is the arms race. Since this is the most serious thing, efforts must be focused on it. Socialist efforts need to become more effective. In order to be effective, efforts should be intense and focused. If you start with ten points at the same time, you disperse your efforts over all these points.

Our efforts must encroach on the bourgeois parties. All these parties see that the army takes the entire budget, and that there's no room for anything else. We will be told: "The homeland is in danger!" We can respond as socialists: "We all have a common homeland." But it's necessary to be practical. By asking merely for a 50 percent decrease, we can say: "You have the means to defend your country." We call for a decrease not just in one country, but in all countries. Fifty percent would be more than enough for conservatives and reactionaries to defend their interests against the people.

It will be said that our resolution must be socialist. But our resolution can only concentrate efforts on one point. It does not stop defending mass movements and making propaganda. The majority's resolution speaks of arbitration courts and other things that have already been spoken of in other countries.

Concentrating our efforts, repeated several times a year in all countries, will be effective. Even for those calling for a general strike, my proposal will be useful. When the time comes for the strike, it will happen more easily due to the propaganda I propose. . . .

Vaillant: I support the majority resolution and will vote for it, but the means are not sufficient. It is necessary to organize efforts by the people. In Stuttgart, we could not do better. Parliamentary action has been indicated, but not action by the proletariat. Parliaments cannot act without the support of the masses. War can be prevented by those who do not want war. The means to be employed can never be too extreme, because it is a question of stopping war. But I agree with Ledebour that we should not list the means so as not to provoke police intervention.

Together with Hardie, I am proposing an amendment to be put at the end of the resolution: "Among the means to be used in order to prevent and hinder war, the Congress considers as particularly effective the general strike, especially in the industries that supply war with its implements (arms and ammunition, transport, etc.), as well as propaganda and popular action in their most active forms."

Keir Hardie (Britain): If our motion is not adopted here, it will be presented before the Congress as a whole. I will not give a speech. If war is declared and if socialist activity in parliament is not enough to stop it, the working class must step in and take extreme measures, including refusing to produce cannons and other war matériel, refusing to run the trains and load coal onto ships. It's clear that a nation would not do this without the agreement of the other belligerent nations. Doing so would be enough to halt hostilities. Rejecting our motion would be rejecting the goal of powerful joint action to prevent war. I therefore ask you to accept the motion.

Dimitrije Tucović (Serbia): . . . The danger of a conflagration is constant in the Balkans. Socialists have fewer reasons to be concerned about the mysteries of diplomacy than in defending small nations that do not wish to be absorbed into the great powers and want to maintain their right to existence. This is a vital position of the socialist parties in small countries. . . . That is why I formulate the following proposal: "The Congress declares that with the aim of energetically fighting colonial policy and conquest in the sense of the Stuttgart resolution, it is necessary that comrades in capitalist nations and states put themselves in touch with the comrades of the oppressed countries that suffer from this policy, with the aim of facilitating the struggle against militarism and chauvinism."

Karl Renner (Austria): I will read a statement by Comrade Radek:

> I have seen that one part of the bourgeois press is writing false interpretations of the remarks I made in the militarism commission. I would like to declare that I obviously never intended to belittle socialist action for peace. On the contrary, I wanted to assure the widest scope of this activity and to expand it, and to bring out that only the revolutionary class struggle is an obstacle to war. I simply wanted to criticize pacifist illusions.

. . . With regard to Tucović's proposal, we have taken it into account in the final part of our resolution, and I ask him not to bring it into the plenary. We cannot codify here all the demands against war. All we can do here is state our agreement. We have our general program, and the program of the different countries.

I cannot support Morgari's resolution. With regard to disarmament, we are unanimously in agreement that we should call for complete disarmament. By that we mean the elimination of all standing armies, but we have no desire to leave the peoples defenseless. . . .

Ledebour: In a conversation with Tucović, he told me that he'd decided to withdraw his proposal. As Renner said, the final part of the amendment takes into account the Serbian proposal. We are completely in agreement with the spirit of that proposal.

Report to Plenary

Georg Ledebour (Germany, reporter): At the international socialist congress in Stuttgart, the question of the stance of socialist parties toward militarism was discussed in the commission for a very long time. At the plenary session a resolution was unanimously adopted indicating the results of the discussions that took place over many days. On the general subject of the socialist stance toward militarism, it explained and formulated our main ideas in a satisfactory manner. But here, as in all other questions of great importance, the question has been illustrated by new facts, which require the congress to take new decisions from a practical point of view.

The events of the last few years provided new incentives to formulate our proposals and submit them to the congress. Two points above all show the possibility of extending the Stuttgart resolution. First, the question of arbitration, in which an important effort is needed. The creation of arbitration courts has always been put forward by bourgeois parties, and especially monarchist parties. Despite that, one can say that the movement for arbitration has been on the decline.

The second element pressing on us is taking a position on the question of dreadnoughts. The construction of these new large battleships—the idea of which originated in Britain—is currently preoccupying all countries, but especially Britain and Germany. This is the biggest threat to world peace. Naval warfare, once considered a secondary question, is now the biggest war danger. In the countries directly concerned, socialists have put forward proposals in parliament. But naturally, international socialism as a whole needs to put forward a unified proposal—as much as possible at the same time—on this question for all countries and states.

I could have limited myself to citing a few facts and avoiding demonstrations of principle on this question. But a well-known socialist like Bruce Glasier, pioneer journalist and intellectual of the ILP, told the commission that the capitalist economic system was not the only cause of war today, but also people's bestial instincts and love of combat. Bruce Glasier was wrong to use such language. It's true that there are bestial instincts of combat found in every individual. But I dispute the fact that this love of combat constitutes, within the capitalist economic organization, a real incitement or appreciable motive for war.

So what actually is the cause of war?

It is the ruling classes, the capitalists, who have an interest in supplying the means of war—Krupp, Tippelskirch, Armstrong, or whatever their name is. These capitalists are not thinking in the slightest of satisfying man's lust for battle or his bestial instincts. Rather, they desire to calmly stay home and rake in the profits resulting from people killing each other. The famous Russian painter Vereshchagin marvelously symbolized this fact in his painting of the battle of Plevna, showing Russian and Turkish people killing each other with weapons of all kinds. In the foreground one sees the tsar of Russia satisfying his spirit of combat and his bestial instincts by emptying glasses of champagne with his generals. [*Laughter and applause*]

It is thus not the spirit of combat that causes modern wars. The culprit is capitalism and its interests. The desire to oppress and exploit foreign peoples—this is the economic cause of modern wars. The rapacity of capitalism has developed powerfully and has made the bourgeoisie forget all of the ideology it displayed in its youth. The only thing that remains is exploitation.

We find an extremely interesting example in the former president of the United States, Mr. [Theodore] Roosevelt, the ideal type of modern capitalist politician in the United States—supposedly the freest country in the world. On all holiday occasions, every capitalist graces himself with phrases about peace and freedom. During Mr. Roosevelt's hunting expedition [in Africa]—not undertaken because of his instinct for combat, but because of his instinct for slaughtering animals—he rudely treated the Egyptians, who it seems are opposed to British oppression and exploitation.[40] This incident is the most conclusive proof of the observation that the ferocious beast of modern capitalist policy stands above all other considerations. [Benjamin] Franklin and [George] Washington, the blessed American defenders of freedom, would certainly have turned over in their graves had they heard the words of their unnatural descendent, the capitalist representative of the American bourgeoisie.

In the commission, we quickly came to agreement on the principles of the declaration. With regard to the specific demands of socialists against capitalist society today, all declarations have been taken into account as much as possible. Only one proposal did not find supporters, that of Citizen Morgari, who proposed that within parliaments of all countries we call for a reduction of the military budget by 50 percent. Comrade Morgari himself declared that he did not insist on the 50 percent figure. He would also settle for 45 percent, and in the end would accept 55 percent of military expenditures. But this socialism of percentages [*laughter*] found no support among the other members of the commission.

Four points of the resolution are taken from delegates' proposals.

First, that demands be put to all parliaments for the creation of permanent and obligatory arbitration courts to resolve international differences. Arbitration councils exist built on the basis of The Hague Conference,[41] but as historical experience shows, never in cases leading to war. Arbitration courts may resolve these conflicts more rapidly. Arbitration courts may bring about the nomination of well-paid diplomats, but these capitalist institutions do not help at all to prevent the danger of war. Whenever "honor" or "vital interests" of a nation are involved, the arbitration court will not make a decision, but will appeal to the *ultima ratio regum*—to the ultimate logic of kings: that is, cannons.

Second, we demand arbitration courts for all international conflicts.

Further, we demand complete disarmament. We attach special importance to the declaration that we strive for complete disarmament, and I was charged by the commission with expressing our gratitude to the Scandinavian comrades, who are marching in the front ranks of socialism and energetically fighting for complete disarmament. . . .

We have also added a fourth point in the resolution, which is not directly related to the war danger but is one of the most dangerous secondary causes of differences among nations and the danger of war. We call for the right of autonomy by all nations and the defense of all countries against military attacks and violent oppression. The small nations above all are interested in the recognition of national autonomy for all peoples of the world.

Germany does not just oppress the Poles and the Danes, but also the French-speaking people of Alsace-Lorraine. On the other hand, there are portions of the German people—two million in Austria and one million in Russia—who are oppressed nationally and linguistically. We call for autonomy for all peoples—and not just in Europe, but also in Asia and Africa.

Socialism is not antinational, as our opponents say, but international, which means something completely different. The nationalist politicians who oppress other nations and do not recognize the rights of their own nation have the most ardent desire to denationalize foreign countries that they dominate owing to geography or conquests. It is this that is antinational. We are international Social Democrats who recognize the right of every mother tongue and every nationality, and we demand that this right be universally recognized. The more this great point of civilization is raised by us in all questions of struggle, the more the peoples will not look to the bourgeois parties, but instead to the socialists. . . .

The Vaillant–Keir Hardie amendment, which you have before you, gave rise to a lively discussion. Here it is. [*Ledebour reads the text of the Vaillant-Hardie amendment.*]

With regard to the means to employ to stop war, the Stuttgart resolution said this:

> In case of war being imminent, the working class and its parliamentary representatives in the countries concerned shall be bound, with the assistance of the International Socialist Bureau, to do all they can to prevent the outbreak of war, using for this purpose the means that appear to them the most effective, and which must naturally vary according to the acuteness of the class struggle and to the general political conditions.

This wording was an extremely happy solution to a thorny question, and it was adopted at Stuttgart unanimously. It does not recognize only the possibility, but also the obligatory need to stop the war danger by extreme means.

But declaring a general strike at all times and in all places—whether it's a general strike before war or when war is declared—that we cannot understand. Economic development in different countries, the strength of Social Democracy, and mainly the different organized forces within the workers' movement make it impossible to give universal prescriptions for a general strike. This does not mean that a general strike is impossible in principle, or that certain circumstances may not arrive making it necessary. But that's different from proclaiming general strikes as a moral duty under all circumstances and in all countries.

If a bourgeois party were to decide to employ "extreme measures" against war, it would mean simply that its supporters would face the threat of war by taking off their felt slippers. The situation is very different for the international proletariat. You can use whatever words you like with all the necessary precautions, but as soon as you accept the expression "general strike" in a resolution, you obligate the proletariat to bring it about. We will not stop at historical considerations; we will tell the proletariat what it has to do.

Think for a moment about the consequences of your acts if you go beyond the Stuttgart resolution. If you want the decisions of the International to be followed everywhere, you will adopt only decisions that can be carried out everywhere. The organizations of every country are not yet strong enough for such a resolution not to have harmful consequences. If you make such a decision, we would have to accept responsibility for all of the consequences. It is the unions that must make the general strike, as you yourselves recognize by citing different groups. . . .

We must enlighten the peoples as to the true nature of militarism. We must protest against the provocation of armaments, because world peace and the welfare of all humanity depend not on naval and land armies, not on monarchies, not on general staffs. Rather, they depend only on the proletariat conscious of the class struggle, on socialists of every country, on their growing confidence and audacity, and on their indefatigable will!

Adopted Resolution

The Congress declares that the armaments of nations have increased alarmingly during recent years in spite of the peace congresses and the protestations of peaceful intentions on the part of the governments. Particularly does this apply to the general movement of the governments to increase naval armaments, whose latest phase is the construction of "dreadnoughts" [battleships]. This policy leads not only to an insane waste of national resources for unproductive purposes—and therefore to the curtailment of means for the realization of necessary social reforms in the interest of the working class—but it also threatens all nations with financial ruin and exhaustion through the unsupportable burdens of indirect taxation.

These armaments have but recently endangered world peace, as they always will. In view of this development, which threatens all the achievements of civilization, the well-being of nations, and the very life of the masses, this Congress reaffirms the resolutions of previous international congresses and particularly that of the Stuttgart Congress.

The workers of all countries have no quarrels or differences that could lead to war. Modern wars are the result of capitalism, and particularly of rivalries of the capitalist classes of the different countries over the world market, and of the spirit of militarism, which is one of the instruments of capitalist class rule and of the economic and political subjugation of the working class. Wars will cease completely only with the disappearance of the capitalist mode of production. The working class, which bears the main burdens of war and suffers most from its effects, has the greatest interest in the prevention of wars. The organized socialist workers of all countries are therefore the only reliable guarantee of universal peace.

The Congress therefore again calls upon the labor organizations of all countries to continue a vigorous propaganda of enlightenment among all workers—and particularly among young people—as to the causes of war, in order to educate them in the spirit of international brotherhood. The Congress, reiterating the oft-repeated duty of socialist representatives in parliament to combat militarism with all means at their command and refusing funds for armaments, requires from its representatives:

(a) To constantly reiterate the demand that international arbitration be made compulsory in all international disputes.

(b) To make persistent and repeated proposals in the direction of ultimate, complete disarmament; and above all, as a first step, the conclusion of a general treaty limiting naval armaments and abrogating the right of seizure at sea.

(c) To demand the abolition of secret diplomacy and the publication of all existing and future agreements between the governments.

(d) To guarantee the self-determination of all nations and their protection from military attacks and forcible subjugation.

The International Socialist Bureau will support all socialist organizations in their fight against militarism by furnishing them with the necessary data and information, and will, when the occasion arrives, endeavor to bring about united action. In case military conflicts arise, this Congress reaffirms the resolution of the Stuttgart Congress, which reads:

> In case of war being imminent, the working class and its parliamentary representatives in the countries concerned shall be bound, with the assistance of the International Socialist Bureau, to do all they can to prevent the outbreak of war, using for this purpose the means that appear to them the most effective and which must naturally vary according to the acuteness of the class struggle and to the general political conditions.
>
> In case war should break out notwithstanding, they shall be bound to intervene for its speedy termination and to employ all their forces to utilize the economic and political crisis created by the war in order to rouse the masses of the people and thereby hasten the downfall of capitalist class rule.

For the proper execution of these measures, the Congress directs the Bureau, in the event of war danger, to take immediate steps to bring about an agreement among the labor parties of the countries affected for united action to prevent the threatened war.

APPENDIX

Lenin on Trends within the Second International

The two articles below present V. I. Lenin's evaluation of the trends in the Second International, as well as of some of the International's key debates recorded in this book. The first article was written immediately following the 1907 Stuttgart Congress. The second article excerpted here was written November 1, 1914, three months after the collapse of the Second International.

Lenin's article on the Stuttgart Congress was published in the underground Bolshevik organ *Proletary*, no. 17, October 20, 1907. He wrote a second version of this article for publication in the legal Russian press. This latter article covers the women's suffrage debate in much greater detail than the original one; for that reason we have replaced the first article's very short account of this debate with the more extensive one from the second article, inserted within brackets.

The texts are taken from Lenin's *Collected Works*.[1]

The International Socialist Congress in Stuttgart (1907)

A feature of the International Socialist Congress held in Stuttgart this August was its large and representative composition: the total of 886 delegates came from all the five continents. Besides providing an impressive demonstration of international unity in the proletarian struggle, the congress played an outstanding part in defining the tactics of the socialist parties. It adopted general resolutions on a number of questions, the decision on which had hitherto been left solely to the discretion of the individual socialist parties. And the fact that more and more problems require uniform, principled decisions in different countries is striking proof that socialism is being welded into a single international force.

The full text of the Stuttgart resolutions will be found elsewhere in this issue. We shall deal briefly with each of them in order to bring out the chief controversial points and the character of the debate at the congress.

This is not the first time the colonial question has figured at international congresses. Up till now their decisions have always been an unqualified condemnation of bourgeois colonial policy as a policy of plunder and violence. This time, however, the congress commission was so composed that opportunist elements, headed by Van Kol of Holland, predominated in it. A sentence was inserted in the draft resolution to the effect that the congress did not in principle condemn all colonial policy, for under socialism colonial policy could play a civilizing role. The minority in the commission (Ledebour of Germany, the Polish and Russian Social Democrats, and many others) vigorously protested against any such idea being entertained. The matter was referred to the congress, where the forces of the two trends were found to be so nearly equal that there was an extremely heated debate.

The opportunists rallied behind Van Kol. Speaking for the majority of the German delegation, Bernstein and David urged acceptance of a "socialist colonial policy" and fulminated against the radicals for their barren, negative attitude, their failure to appreciate the importance of reforms, their lack of a practical colonial program, etc. Incidentally, they were opposed by Kautsky, who felt compelled to ask the congress to pronounce *against* the majority of the German delegation. He rightly pointed out that there was no question of rejecting the struggle for reforms; that was explicitly stated in other sections of the resolution, which had evoked no dispute. The point at issue was whether we should make concessions to the modern regime of bourgeois plunder and violence. The congress was to discuss present-day colonial policy, which was based on the downright enslavement of primitive populations. The bourgeoisie was actually introducing slavery in the colonies and subjecting the native populations to unprecedented outrages and acts of violence, "civilizing" them by the spread of liquor and syphilis. And in that situation socialists were expected to utter evasive phrases about the possibility of accepting colonial policy in principle! That would be an outright desertion to the bourgeois point of view. It would be a decisive step towards subordinating the proletariat to bourgeois ideology, to bourgeois imperialism, which is now arrogantly raising its head.

The congress defeated the commission's motion by 128 votes to 108 with 10 abstentions (Switzerland). It should be noted that at Stuttgart, for the first time, each nation was allotted a definite number of votes, varying from twenty (for the big nations, Russia included) to two (Luxembourg). The combined vote of the small nations, which either do not pursue a colonial policy, or which suffer from it, outweighed the vote of nations where even the proletariat has been somewhat infected with the lust of conquest.

This vote on the colonial question is of very great importance. First, it strikingly showed up socialist opportunism, which succumbs to bourgeois blandishments. Secondly, it revealed a negative feature in the European labor movement, one that can do no little harm to the proletarian cause and for that reason should receive serious attention. Marx frequently quoted a very significant saying of Sismondi. The proletarians of the ancient world, this saying runs, lived at the expense of society; modern society lives at the expense of the proletarians.[2]

The nonpropertied, but nonworking, class is incapable of overthrowing the exploiters. Only the proletarian class, which maintains the whole of society, can bring about the social revolution. However, as a result of the extensive colonial policy, the European proletarian *partly* finds himself in a position when it is *not* his labor, but the labor of the practically enslaved natives in the colonies, that maintains the whole of society. The British bourgeoisie, for example, derives more profit from the many millions of the population of India and other colonies than from the British workers. In certain countries this provides the material and economic basis for infecting the proletariat with colonial chauvinism. Of course, this may be only a temporary phenomenon, but the evil must nonetheless be clearly realized and its causes understood in order to be able to rally the proletariat of all countries for the struggle against such opportunism. This struggle is bound to be victorious, since the "privileged" nations are a diminishing faction of the capitalist nations.

[The resolution on women's suffrage was adopted unanimously.[3] Only one Englishwoman from the semi-bourgeois Fabian Society defended the admissibility of a struggle not for full women's suffrage but for one limited to those possessing property. The congress rejected this unconditionally and declared in favor of women workers campaigning for the franchise, not in conjunction with the bourgeois supporters of women's rights, but in conjunction with the class parties of the proletariat. The congress recognized that in the campaign for women's suffrage it was necessary to uphold fully the principles of socialism and equal rights for men and women without distorting those principles for the sake of expediency.

[In this connection, an interesting difference of opinion arose in the commission. The Austrians (Victor Adler, Adelheid Popp) justified their tactics in the struggle for universal manhood suffrage: for the sake of winning this suffrage, they thought it expedient in their campaign not to put the demand for women's suffrage, too, in the foreground. The German Social Democrats, and especially Clara Zetkin, had protested against this when the Austrians were campaigning for universal suffrage. Zetkin declared in the press that they should not under any circumstances have neglected the demand for women's suffrage, that the Austrians had opportunistically sacrificed principle to expediency, and that they would not have narrowed the scope of their agitation, but would have widened it and increased the force of the popular movement had they fought for women's suffrage with the same energy.

In the commission, Zetkin was supported wholeheartedly by another prominent German woman Social Democrat, [Luise] Zietz. Adler's amendment, which indirectly justified the Austrian tactics, was *rejected* by 12 votes to 9 (this amendment stated only that there should be no abatement of the struggle for a suffrage that would really extend to all citizens, instead of stating that the struggle for suffrage should always include the demand for equal rights for men and women). The point of view of the commission and of the congress may be most accurately expressed in the following words of the above-mentioned Zietz in her speech at the International Socialist Women's Conference (this conference took place in Stuttgart at the same time as the congress):

["In principle, we must demand all that we consider to be correct," said Zietz, "and only when our strength is inadequate for more, do we accept what we are able to get. That has always been the tactics of Social Democracy. The more modest our demands, the more modest will the government be in its concessions. . . ." This controversy between the Austrian and German women Social Democrats will enable the reader to see how severely the best Marxists treat the slightest deviation from the principles of consistent revolutionary tactics.][4] . . .

A few words about the resolution on emigration and immigration. Here, too, in the commission there was an attempt to defend narrow, craft interests, to ban the immigration of workers from backward countries (coolies—from China, etc.). This is the same spirit of aristocratism that one finds among workers in some of the "civilized" countries, who derive certain advantages from their privileged position and are therefore inclined to forget the need for international class solidarity. But no one at the congress defended this craft and petty-bourgeois narrow-mindedness. The resolution fully meets the demands of revolutionary Social Democracy.

We pass now to the last, and perhaps the most important, resolution of the congress—that on antimilitarism. The notorious Hervé, who has made such a noise in France and Europe, advocated a semi-anarchist view by naively suggesting that every war be "answered" by a strike and an uprising. He did not understand, on the one hand, that war is a necessary product of capitalism, and that the proletariat cannot renounce participation in revolutionary wars, for such wars are possible, and have indeed occurred in capitalist societies. He did not understand, on the other hand, that the possibility of "answering" a war depends on the nature of the crisis created by that war. The choice of the means of struggle depends on these conditions; moreover, the struggle must consist (and here we have the third misconception, or shallow thinking of Hervéism) not simply in replacing war by peace, but in replacing capitalism by socialism. The essential thing is not merely to prevent war, but to utilize the crisis created by war in order to hasten the overthrow of the bourgeoisie. However, underlying all these semi-anarchist absurdities of Hervéism there was one sound and practical purpose: to spur the socialist movement so that it will not be restricted to parliamentary methods of struggle alone, so that the masses will realize the need for revolutionary action in connection with the crises which war inevitably involves, so that, lastly, a more lively understanding of international labor solidarity and of the falsity of bourgeois patriotism will be spread among the masses.

Bebel's resolution (moved by the Germans and coinciding in all essentials with Guesde's resolution) had one shortcoming—it failed to indicate the active tasks of the proletariat. This made it possible to read Bebel's orthodox propositions through opportunist spectacles, and Vollmar was quick to turn this possibility into a reality.

That is why Rosa Luxemburg and the Russian Social Democratic delegates moved their amendments to Bebel's resolution. These amendments: (1) stated that militarism is the chief weapon of class oppression; (2) pointed out the need for propaganda among the youth; (3) stressed that Social Democrats should not only try to prevent war from breaking out or to secure the speediest termination of wars that have already begun, but should utilize the crisis created by the war to hasten the overthrow of the bourgeoisie.

The subcommission (elected by the antimilitarism commission) incorporated all these amendments in Bebel's resolution. In addition, Jaurès made this happy suggestion: instead of enumerating the methods of struggle (strikes, uprisings) the resolution should cite historical examples of proletarian action against war, from the demonstrations in Europe to the revolution in Russia. The result of all this redrafting was a resolution which, it is true, is unduly long, but is rich in thought and precisely formulates the tasks of the proletariat. It combines the stringency of orthodox—i.e., the only scientific Marxist analysis with recommendations for the most resolute and revolutionary action by the workers' parties. This resolution cannot be interpreted à la Vollmar, nor can it be fitted into the narrow framework of naive Hervéism.

On the whole, the Stuttgart Congress brought into sharp contrast the opportunist and revolutionary wings of the international Social Democratic movement on a number of cardinal issues and decided these issues in the spirit of revolutionary Marxism. Its resolutions and the report of the debates should become a handbook for every propagandist. The work done at Stuttgart will greatly promote the unity of tactics and unity of revolutionary struggle of the proletarians of all countries.

The Position and Tasks of the Socialist International (1914)

The gravest feature of the present crisis is that the majority of official representatives of European socialism have succumbed to bourgeois nationalism, to chauvinism. It is with good reason that the bourgeois press of all countries writes of them now with derision, now with condescending praise. To anyone who wants to remain a socialist, there can be no more important duty than to reveal the causes of this crisis in socialism and analyze the tasks of the International.

There are those who are afraid to admit that the crisis or, to put it more accurately, the collapse of the Second International, is the collapse of opportunism.

Reference is made to the unanimity, for instance, among French socialists, and to the fact that the old groups in socialism have supposedly changed their stances on the question of the war. Such references, however, are groundless.

Advocacy of class collaboration; abandonment of the idea of socialist revolution and revolutionary methods of struggle; adaptation to bourgeois nationalism; losing sight of the fact that the borderlines of nationality and country are historically transient; making a fetish of bourgeois legality; renunciation of the class viewpoint and the class struggle, for fear of repelling the "broad masses of the population" (meaning the petty bourgeoisie)—such, doubtlessly, are the ideological foundations of opportunism. And it is from such soil that the present chauvinist and patriotic frame of mind of most Second International leaders has developed. Observers representing the most varied points of view have long noted that the opportunists are in fact prevalent in the Second International's leadership. The war has merely brought out, rapidly and saliently, the true measure of this prevalence. There is nothing surprising in the extraordinary acuteness of the crisis having led to a series of reshufflings within the old groups. On the whole, however, such changes have affected only individuals. The trends within socialism have remained the same.[5] . . .

The collapse of the International is a fact. It has been proved conclusively by the polemic, in the press, between the French and German socialists, and acknowledged, not only by the Left Social Democrats (Mehring and *Bremer Bürger-Zeitung*), but by moderate Swiss papers (*Volksrecht*). Kautsky's attempts to cover up this collapse are a cowardly subterfuge. The collapse of the International is clearly the collapse of opportunism, which is now captive to the bourgeoisie.

The bourgeoisie's stance is clear. It is no less clear that the opportunists are simply echoing bourgeois arguments. In addition to what has been said in the leading article, we need only mention the insulting statements in *Die Neue Zeit*, suggesting that internationalism consists in the workers of one country shooting down the workers of another country, allegedly in defense of the fatherland!

The question of the fatherland—we shall reply to the opportunists—cannot be posed without due consideration of the concrete historical nature of the present war. This is an imperialist war, i.e., it is being waged at a time of the highest development of capitalism, a time of its approaching end. The working class must first "constitute itself within the nation," the Communist Manifesto declares, emphasizing the limits and conditions of our recognition of nationality and fatherland as essential forms of the bourgeois system, and, consequently, of the bourgeois fatherland. The opportunists distort that truth by extending to the period of the end of capitalism that which was true of the period of its rise. With reference to the former period and to the tasks of the proletariat in its struggle to destroy not feudalism but capitalism, the Communist Manifesto gives a clear and precise formula: "The workingmen have no country." One can well understand why the opportunists are so afraid to accept this socialist proposition, afraid even, in most cases, to openly reckon with it. The socialist movement cannot triumph within the old framework of the fatherland. It creates new and superior forms of human society, in which the legitimate needs and progressive aspirations of the working masses of *each* nationality will, for the first time, be met through international unity, provided existing national partitions are removed. To the present-day bourgeoisie's attempts to divide and disunite them by means of hypocritical appeals for the "defense of the fatherland," the class-conscious workers will reply with ever new and persevering efforts to unite the workers of various nations in the struggle to overthrow the rule of the bourgeoisie of all nations.

The bourgeoisie is duping the masses by disguising imperialist rapine with the old ideology of a "national war." This deceit is being shown up by the proletariat, which has brought forward its slogan of turning the imperialist war into a civil war. This was the slogan of the Stuttgart and Basel resolutions, which had in mind, not war in general, but precisely the present war and spoke, not of "defense of the fatherland," but of "hastening the downfall of capitalism," of utilizing the war-created crisis for this purpose, and of the example provided by the Paris Commune. The latter was an instance of a war of nations being turned into a civil war. . . .

The Second International is dead, overcome by opportunism. Down with opportunism, and long live the Third International, purged not only of "turncoats" (as *Golos* wishes), but of opportunism as well.

The Second International did its share of useful preparatory work in preliminarily organizing the proletarian masses during the long, "peaceful" period of the most brutal capitalist slavery and most rapid capitalist progress in the last third of the nineteenth and the beginning of the twentieth centuries. To the Third International falls the task of organizing the proletarian forces for a revolutionary onslaught against the capitalist governments, for civil war against the bourgeoisie of all countries for the capture of political power, for the triumph of socialism!

Glossary

Adler, Victor (1852–1918) – founder and central leader of Austrian Social Democratic Workers Party 1888–1918; prominent leader of Second International; supported Austro-Hungarian military effort in World War I; Austrian foreign minister 1918.

Armstrong – presumed reference to Sir W. G. Armstrong Whitworth & Co Ltd., a major world armaments manufacturer.

Auer, Ignaz (1846–1907) – joined German Social Democratic Workers Party 1866; secretary of SPD Executive 1890–94; coeditor of *Vorwärts*; member of Reichstag several times between 1878 and 1906; supporter of party's reformist wing.

Aveling, Edward (1849–1898) – British socialist; joined Social Democratic Federation 1884; left SDF to help found Socialist League, belonging to it until 1886; rejoined SDF 1896; a translator of Marx.

Babeuf, François-Noël (Gracchus) (1760–1797) – French revolutionary and early communist; advocated abolition of private property; leader of "Conspiracy of the Equals"; arrested, tried, and executed.

Bebel, August (1840–1913) – a founder of German Social Democratic Workers Party 1869; collaborator of Marx and Engels; SPD cochair from 1892 until his death; opposed revisionism in SPD and Second International but came to adopt centrist position.

Bernstein, Eduard (1850–1932) – joined German Social Democratic Workers Party 1872; collaborator of Engels and Kautsky; theorist of revisionist current within SPD from 1898; member of centrist Independent

Social Democratic Party (USPD) during World War I; rejoined SPD 1919; Reichstag deputy 1902–07, 1912–18, 1920–28.

Bismarck, Otto von (1815–1898) – German politician and writer; prime minister of Prussia from 1862; collaborated in crushing Paris Commune 1871; first chancellor of German Empire 1871–90; sponsor of Anti-Socialist Laws 1878–90.

Blanqui, Louis-Auguste (1805–1881) – French proletarian revolutionist; spent over thirty-three years in prison; associated with strategy of armed insurrection by small groups.

Bracke, Alexandre (1861–1955) – joined French socialist movement in 1880s, becoming leader of French SP; party foreign relations secretary; longtime member of Chamber of Deputies; supported French military effort during World War I.

Branting, Karl Hjalmar (1860–1925) – longtime leader of Swedish Social Democratic Party and editor of *Social-Demokraten* 1886–1917; supporter of Bernstein's revisionist perspective; opponent of Bolshevik revolution; chairperson of Second International 1919; three times prime minister 1920–25.

Bülow, Prince Bernhard von (1849–1929) – German foreign minister 1897–1900; chancellor 1900–09.

Buonarroti, Philippe (Filippo) (1761–1837) – Italian-born French revolutionary; collaborator of Babeuf in "Conspiracy of the Equals"; later participated in radical republican opposition to Bonapartist and restoration regimes.

Burrows, Herbert (1845–1922) – British socialist; founding member in 1881 of organization that became Social Democratic Federation, remaining a member until 1911.

Bund – General Union of Jewish Workers in Lithuania, Poland, and Russia; founded in tsarist Russian Empire 1897; affiliated to Russian Social Democratic Labor Party 1898–1903 and from 1906, siding with Mensheviks; opposed October Revolution; left wing split in 1919 and became Communist Bund; social democratic wing functioned as separate organization outside Soviet Union.

Cama, Bhikaiji (Madam Cama) (1861–1936) – Indian independence advocate; lived in Paris from 1905; a founder of Indian Home Rule Society and Paris Indian Society; addressed Second International's 1907 Stuttgart Congress; supporter of women's equality; deported to Martinique during World War I, returning to Paris afterward.

Chamberlain, Joseph (1836–1914) – British secretary of state for the colonies 1895–1903; promoted schemes to expand British Empire.

Cocea, Nicolae Dumitru (1880–1949) – Romanian journalist, novelist, and political activist; joined socialist movement early 1900s; delegate to Second International's Copenhagen Congress 1910; supporter of Russian Revolution and Communist movement; vice president of Romanian Writers' Union after World War II.

Combes, Émile (1835–1921) – member of French Radical Party; prime minister 1902–05.

Compère-Morel, Adéodat (1872–1941) – joined French socialist movement 1891; secretary of French Workers Party (POF) and then a leader of Socialist Party of France (PSDF) and unified SP (SFIO); delegate to 1907 Stuttgart Congress; parliamentary deputy 1909–36; leader of SP right wing that broke with party when it became CP in 1920.

David, Eduard (1863–1930) – joined German Social Democratic Party early 1890s; member of Reichstag from 1903; right-wing SPD leader; widely published propagandist for majority policy during World War I; minister in SPD-led government 1919–20; first president of National Assembly 1919.

De Leon, Daniel (1852–1914) – joined US Socialist Labor Party 1890; editor of its newspaper *The People*; central leader of SLP until his death.

Delescluze, Charles (1809–1871) – French revolutionary; founder of *Le Réveil*; elected official in Paris Commune; member of Committee of Public Safety; killed in battle while defending Commune.

Dessin, Alexander Hermann Max (1862–1926) – born in Germany; emigrated to Bradford in England; secondary school language teacher; delegate from Social Democratic Federation to 1910 Copenhagen Congress; close associate of Hyndman.

Diner-Dénes, József (1857–1937) – Hungarian writer and journalist; leading Social Democrat; editor of *Munka Szemléje* [Labor Review] 1906–10; appointed foreign secretary in Hungarian government 1918; later lived in Paris and worked for social democratic *Le Populaire*.

Ellenbogen, Wilhelm (1863–1951) – founding member and prominent leader of Austrian Social Democratic Workers Party; member of parliament 1901–18; took pacifist position during World War I; participated in Zimmerwald Movement; entered Social Democratic–led Austrian government in 1919.

Engels, Frederick (1820–1895) – lifelong collaborator of Karl Marx; coauthor of Communist Manifesto; a leader of First International 1864–72; political and theoretical leader of revolutionary workers' movement after death of Marx; close adviser of Second International 1889–95.

Fabian Society – liberal-reformist British organization; affiliated to Second International.

Ferri, Enrico (1856–1929) – Italian criminologist and socialist; joined Italian SP 1893; elected to Italian parliament 1896; editor of *Avanti* 1900–05; became supporter of fascism under Mussolini.

Fischer, Richard (1855–1926) – joined social democratic movement in Switzerland 1876; moved back to Germany and became SPD member; party secretary 1890–93; Reichstag deputy 1893–1918; member of SPD Executive.

French Socialist Party (PSF) – formed 1902 by fusion of reformist currents; most prominent leader was Jean Jaurès; fused with Socialist Party of France (PSDF) to form unified SP (SFIO) in 1905.

French Workers Party (POF) – Marxist party created 1880 by Jules Guesde and Paul Lafargue; combated reformist currents in French workers' movement; merged in 1901 with Blanquist forces to form Socialist Party of France (PSDF); part of 1905 merger with French Socialist Party (PSF) to form unified SP (SFIO).

Furnémont, Léon (1861–1927) – joined Belgian Workers Party 1893; socialist councilor in Brussels until 1903; member of parliament 1894–1913.

Galliffet, Gaston, Marquis de (1830–1909) – French general notorious for summary execution of thousands after fall of Paris Commune 1871; in 1899–1900 was war minister in Waldeck-Roussseau cabinet, which also included Millerand.

Glasier, Bruce (1859–1920) – joined Social Democratic Federation in Scotland 1882; left SDF for Socialist League 1885; joined Independent Labour Party 1893; party chairman 1900–03; editor of *Labour Leader* 1905–09; took pacifist stand during World War I, opposing British involvement.

Golos (The Voice) – daily Menshevik paper, published in Paris from September 1914 to January 1915.

Guesde, Jules (1845–1922) – one of first Marxists in France; from 1882 leader of French Workers Party (POF) and French SP (SFIO); opponent of reformism until 1914; social patriot and minister without portfolio during World War I.

Hammer, Julius (1874–1948) – represented US Socialist Labor Party at 1907 Stuttgart Congress; later member of left wing of SP and founding member of Communist Labor Party in 1919.

Hardie, Keir (1856–1915) – founding member of British Independent Labour Party, becoming a central party leader; a founder of Labour Party; member of Parliament 1892–95, 1900–15; adopted pacifist stand during World War I.

Hervé, Gustave (1871–1944) – joined French socialist movement 1899; led ultraleft tendency in SP before 1914; became prowar ultranationalist in 1914; expelled from SP 1916; sympathetic to fascism in 1920s; supported Vichy regime during World War II.

Hillquit, Morris (1869–1933) – a founder and central leader of Socialist Party of America from 1901; proponent of opportunist position on immigration and other questions; supporter of centrist current within international Social Democracy.

Hyndman, Henry M. (1842–1921) – a founder in 1881 of what became Social Democratic Federation; helped establish British Socialist Party in 1911; noted for anti-Semitic views; supported British war effort during World War I; formed National Socialist Party in 1916.

L'Humanité – French daily socialist newspaper established 1904 by Jean Jaurès; became organ of SP and later CP.

Iglesias, Pablo (1850–1925) – founder of Spanish Social Democracy 1879; president of SP 1888–1925; head of trade union federation; member of parliament 1910–23; supported Entente during World War I.

Independent Labour Party (ILP) – British social democratic party formed 1893; played leading role in formation of Labour Party, affiliating to it 1906–32.

Jaurès, Jean (1859–1914) – socialist from late 1880s; leader of reformist wing of French socialist movement; from 1905 a central leader of unified French SP (SFIO); member of Chamber of Deputies 1888–89, 1893–98, 1902–14; founder of *L'Humanité* 1904; assassinated at outbreak of World War I.

Kahan – a reference to either Boris or Zelda Kahan. **Boris Kahan** (1877–1951) was born in Kiev; joined East London Jewish branch of Social Democratic Federation 1904 and became its secretary; delegate to 1907 Stuttgart Congress. **Zelda Kahan** (1886–1969) joined Social Democratic Federation 1904; active in its Hackney and Kingsland branches; delegate to 1907 Stuttgart Congress; elected to British Socialist Party executive committee 1912; later member of Communist Party.

Karski – See Marchlewski, Julian.

Kato Tokijiro (1858–1930) – Japanese physician trained in Germany; member of Japanese Socialist Party at 1907 Stuttgart Congress.

Kautsky, Karl (1854–1938) – joined Austrian Social Democracy 1874; collaborator of Engels; moved to Germany and was chief editor of SPD journal *Die Neue Zeit* 1883–1917; prominent Marxist theorist and opponent of revisionism before 1914; centrist during World War I; opponent of October 1917 Russian Revolution and Communist movement.

Klein, Nicholas (1884–1951) – socialist journalist, politician, and lawyer from Cincinnati; traveled around Midwest as Socialist Party speaker and organizer in early 1900s; author of socialist children's primer; became opponent of socialism in 1920s; later served as vice mayor of Cincinnati.

Knudsen, Peter (1848–1910) – leader of Danish Social Democratic Party from 1882 until his death; member of parliament 1891–1901, 1902–09.

Kough, Kathleen B. (1870–1964) – joined Social Democratic Federation in Manchester around 1905; active in SDF Women's Committee and votes-for-women movement as member of Adult Suffrage Society.

Kroemer, Victor (1883–1930) – active in Victoria Socialist Party in South Australia, which in 1907 affiliated to Socialist Federation of Australasia; delegate to 1907 Stuttgart Congress; became a spiritualist following outbreak of World War I.

Krupp – German armaments manufacturing dynasty.

Lassalle, Ferdinand (1825–1864) – participant in 1848–49 revolution in Germany; founder and first president of General German Workers Association 1863; campaigner for suffrage and workers' rights; killed in duel; followers joined with Marxists in 1875 to form what became SPD.

Lawrence, A. H. (1881–1949) – leader of Independent Labour Party from Sunderland in northern England; worked as machinist in iron foundry; represented ILP and Fabian Society at 1907 Stuttgart Congress; member of congress's colonial commission.

Ledebour, Georg (1850–1947) – joined German Social Democratic Party 1891; Reichstag member 1900–18; supported SPD left wing before 1914; opposed social chauvinism during World War I; a leader of Independent Social Democratic Party (USPD) 1917–19; opposed affiliation to Communist International 1920.

Lenin, Vladimir Ilyich (1870–1924) – became active in Russian Social Democratic movement 1892–93; central leader of Bolsheviks from 1903; became Bolshevik representative on International Socialist Bureau for most of 1905-12 period; leader of October 1917 Revolution; chair of Soviet government 1917–24; founder and leader of Communist International.

Liebknecht, Karl (1871–1919) – joined German SPD 1900; first president of Socialist Youth International 1907–10; convicted of treason in 1907 for his book *Militarism and Anti-Militarism*; imprisoned eighteen months; first member of German Reichstag to vote against war credits December 1914; a founder of Spartacus current; a leader of German CP at its founding December 1918; murdered by rightist officers during January 1919 Berlin workers' uprising; son of Wilhelm Liebknecht.

Liebknecht, Wilhelm (1826–1900) – participant in 1848 revolution in Germany; collaborator of Marx and Engels; cofounder of German Social Democracy 1869 and, with Bebel, leader of SPD until his death; chief editor of *Vorwärts* 1876–78 and 1891–1900.

Lucas, Mark (c. 1878–?) – born in England; worked as engraver; after moving to Johannesburg, he participated in founding Transvaal Independent Labour Party 1906, becoming its general treasurer; selected as delegate of South African Socialist Federation to 1907 Stuttgart Congress.

Luxemburg, Rosa (1871–1919) – born in Poland; joined socialist movement 1886; later lived in Germany; delegate to all Second International congresses between 1896 and 1912; led SPD left wing in opposition to party right wing and, after 1910, against "Marxist Center" led by Kautsky; leader of Spartacus current during World War I; imprisoned 1916–18; founding leader of German CP December 1918; arrested and murdered by rightist officers during January 1919 Berlin workers' uprising.

MacDonald, Ramsay (1866–1937) – joined Independent Labour Party 1894; elected to Parliament for Labour Party 1906; British prime minister 1924, 1929–35.

Malecki. Presumably a reference to Henryk Walecki (see entry).

Marchlewski, Julian (Karski) (1866–1925) – joined Social Democratic movement in Russian Poland 1889; joined Bolsheviks 1906; later active in German SPD; during World War I participated in Spartacus group; played a leading role in Communist International.

Martov, Julius (1873–1923) – joined Russian social democratic movement by 1892; leader of Mensheviks from 1903; pacifist during World War I; in left wing of Mensheviks during 1917; opponent of October Revolution.

Marx, Karl (1818–1883) – cofounder with Engels of modern communist workers' movement; leader of Communist League 1847–52; coauthor of Communist Manifesto; central leader of First International 1864–72.

McMillan, Margaret (1860–1931) – British nursery school pioneer; joined socialist movement around 1889, belonging to Fabian Society, SDF, and ILP; active in Labour Party from 1902; participant in women's suffrage fight.

Mehring, Franz (1846–1919) – became German radical democrat in 1870s, sympathetic to Lassalleanism; won to Marxism and joined SPD 1891; chief editor of *Leipziger Volkszeitung* 1902–07; a leading contributor to *Die Neue Zeit*; close collaborator of Rosa Luxemburg from 1912; founding member of Spartacus current 1914–15, and CP 1918.

Millerand, Alexandre (1859–1943) – initially a member of Independent Socialist group in French parliament; took ministerial post in cabinet 1899 and then moved to right of bourgeois political spectrum; French premier 1920; president 1920–24.

Moor, Karl (1852–1932) – joined German Social Democrats in 1870s; expelled from Germany; a leader of Swiss Social Democracy and editor of *Berner Tagwacht*; became Communist after Russian Revolution.

Morgari, Oddino (1865–1944) – joined Italian SP 1891; became chief editor of *Avanti* 1908; parliamentary deputy 1897–1929; member of International Socialist Committee elected at Zimmerwald Conference; later became a leader of reformist SP.

Murby, Millicent (1873–1951) – joined British Fabian Society 1901; served on its national executive committee 1907–12; founding member and leader of Fabian Women's Group.

Die Neue Zeit (New Times)– theoretical journal of German Social Democratic Party, published in Stuttgart, monthly 1883–90, weekly 1890–1923; edited by Kautsky up to 1917.

Nieuwenhuis, Ferdinand Domela (1846–1919) – Dutch former Lutheran minister; joined socialist movement 1879; secretary of Social Democratic League 1882–87; member of parliament 1888–91; moved toward anarchism and advocated general strike against war at 1891 and 1893 Second International congresses; left Social Democratic League 1898; helped found International Antimilitarist Association 1904.

Paeplow, Fritz (1860–1934) – joined SPD late 1880s; member of executive committee of General Commission of German Trade Unions 1899–1902; president of construction workers' union 1913–27.

Pelletier, Madeleine (1874–1939) – became feminist and socialist by 1900; led La Solidarité des Femmes (Women's Solidarity) 1906–12; member of French SP's Permanent Administrative Council 1909–11;

founded and directed *La Suffragiste* 1907–14; member of Communist Party 1920–26.

Pernerstorfer, Engelbert (1850–1918) – joined Austrian Social Democratic Workers Party 1896; member of parliament 1885–97, 1901–18, becoming head of party's parliamentary group.

Plekhanov, Georgy V. (1856–1918) – pioneer of Marxism in Russia; founder of Emancipation of Labor group 1883; supported Mensheviks after 1903; leading Russian representative at Second International congresses; supported Russian military effort during World War I; opposed 1917 October Revolution.

Popp, Adelheid (1869–1939) – Austrian feminist and socialist; joined Social Democratic Workers Party after 1889 and became party's leading female member; editor in chief of its women's newspaper, *Der Arbeiterinnenzeitung*; elected to parliament 1919.

Quelch, Harry (1858–1913) – leader of British Social Democratic Federation and British Socialist Party; editor of *Justice*, 1892–1913; attended all congresses of Second International from 1889 to 1910.

Radek, Karl (1885–1939) – joined revolutionary movement in Austrian Poland before 1905; a leader of left wing of Polish and German workers' movement; internationalist during World War I; joined Bolsheviks 1917; member of Russian CP Central Committee 1917–24; member of Comintern Executive Committee 1920–24 and its Presidium 1921–24; with Trotsky, a leader of Left Opposition in Russian CP and Comintern from 1923; expelled and exiled 1927; capitulated 1929; arrested 1936; convicted in Moscow trial 1937; exiled to labor camp; murdered by a prisoner instigated by secret police.

Rakovsky, Christian (1873–1941) – born in Bulgaria; driven into exile 1890, joining socialist movement in Switzerland; leading socialist activist in several European countries; took part in Zimmerwald Conference 1915; joined Bolsheviks in Russia 1917; leader of Ukrainian soviet government 1919–23; leader of Left Opposition in Russian CP 1923–34; convicted in Moscow frame-up trial 1938; executed.

Rappoport, Charles (1865–1941) – born in Lithuania; joined Russian populist movement 1883; in exile from 1887; joined French socialist movement 1897; member of French CP 1920–38.

Renner, Karl (1870–1950) – joined Austrian Social Democratic Workers Party 1896; prominent revisionist; supported Austro-Hungarian effort in World War I; Austrian chancellor 1918–20, 1945; president of Austria 1945–50.

Roosevelt, Theodore (1858–1919) – US president 1901–09.

Rouanet, Gustave (1855–1927) – joined French socialist movement 1870s; founder of *La revue socialiste* 1885; socialist deputy from Paris 1893–1914; supported French war effort in World War I; opposed Communists in 1920 party split.

SFIO (French Section of the Workers' International) – formed 1905 as fusion of parties led by Guesde-Vaillant and by Jaurès; seventy-three thousand members in 1914; chauvinist position during World War I; voted to join Comintern in 1920 and change name to Communist Party; minority split off and retained old name.

Shaw, Charles Nathaniel Lowe (1877–1960) – born in Ireland, moving to England in 1901; became prominent socialist speaker and writer; delegate to 1907 Stuttgart Congress representing *Clarion* socialist journal and Clarion Scouts, a socialist scouting movement for young people; later emphasized belief in spiritualism and withdrew from socialist movement.

Simons, Algie Martin (1870–1950) – joined US Socialist Labor Party 1897; helped found SP 1901; editor of *International Socialist Review* 1900–08; supported US entry into World War I; later became supporter of Republican Party.

Smart, Russell (1858–1923) – a leader of Independent Labour Party in Britain from mid-1890s; editor of *ILP News*; developed differences with ILP and participated in founding British Socialist Party 1911; resigned from BSP 1912.

Social Democratic Federation (SDF) – British organization founded as Democratic Federation 1881, changing name in 1884; led by Hyndman; fused with other currents into British Socialist Party 1911.

Social Democratic Party of Germany (SPD) – founded 1875 from fusion of Marxist Social Democratic Workers Party and Lassallean General German Workers Association; central party of Second International; majority leadership backed German war effort 1914; left-wing oppositionists formed Spartacus League 1916 and Independent Social Democratic Party (USPD) 1917; headed restabilization of German capitalist rule after November 1918 revolution.

Socialist Labor Party (United States) – founded 1876; in 1890 Daniel De Leon assumed leadership and party adopted sectarian stance.

Socialist Party of America – founded 1901; membership of 30,000 in 1907, 120,000 in 1912; communist left wing expelled 1919.

Socialist Party of France (PSDF) – formed in 1901 by fusion of French Workers Party led by Guesde and Socialist Revolutionary Party led by Vaillant; fused with French Socialist Party (PSF) to form unified SP (SFIO) in 1905.

Südekum, Albert (1871–1944) – joined German Social Democratic Party early 1890s; editor of SPD newspapers and journals; member of party right wing; from 1900 a member of Reichstag; worked with German foreign office during World War I; Prussian finance minister 1918–20.

Terwagne, Modeste (1864–1945) – joined Belgian Workers Party 1894 and became leader of party in Antwerp; member of parliament 1900–19; headed government propaganda agency during World War I; led right-wing split from party after war.

Tirpitz, Alfred von (1849–1930) – German admiral; secretary of state of German Imperial Naval Office 1897–1916.

Tokijiro, Kato. See Kato Tokijiro

Tucović, Dimitrije (1881–1914) – a founder of Serbian Social Democratic Party 1903; editor of party newspapers and journals; enlisted in Serbian army after onset of World War I; killed in battle.

Ugarte, Manuel (1875–1951) – joined Argentine Socialist Party 1903; left it 1913 due to party's rightist positions; a supporter of Latin American anti-imperialist movements; Argentine ambassador under Perón 1946–50.

Uhry, Jules (1877–1936) – French lawyer; joined socialist student movement 1895; member of French Socialist Party led by Jaurès at its founding in 1902; judicial editor of *L'Humanité*; supporter of French efforts in World War I; opponent of Communists in 1920 party split.

Vaillant, Édouard (1840–1915) – joined First International in 1860s, serving on its General Council; participant in Paris Commune 1871; in exile 1872–80; member of Blanquist wing of French socialist movement; a leader of unified French SP after its 1905 fusion; prominent antimilitarist favoring general strike to oppose war; supported French war effort 1914.

Valär, Giovanni (1864–1942) – born in Switzerland, went to school in Italy; forced into exile in 1899 due to political repression; active in Italian immigrant workers' movement in Germany; edited *L'Operaio italiano*, published by trade unions in Hamburg aimed at immigrant workers; later lived in Italy, Switzerland, and Germany; forced to flee Nazis 1933; remained active in Italian Socialist Party.

Vandervelde, Émile (1866–1938) – joined Belgian Workers Party 1889, becoming a central leader; chairperson of Brussels office of Second International 1900–14; member of Belgian council of ministers 1916–21, 1925–27, 1936–37; chairperson of Belgian Workers Party 1933–38.

Van Kol, Hendrick (1852–1925) – member of First International; lived many years in Dutch East Indies from 1876; founding leader of Dutch Social Democratic Workers Party 1894; member of parliament 1897–1909, 1913–22, and 1923–24; prominent opportunist on colonial and other questions within Second International.

Vereshchagin, Vasily Vasilyevich (1842–1904) – Russian artist, noted for graphic war paintings.

Vliegen, Willem Hubertus (1862–1947) – joined Dutch Social Democracy 1883; a leader of right wing in Social Democratic Workers Party through 1930s; member of immigration commission at 1907 Stuttgart Congress.

Vollmar, Georg von (1850–1922) – former German army officer in Franco-Prussian War; won to Social Democracy 1872; member of Reichstag 1881–87 and 1890–1918; first open advocate of revisionism in SPD 1890; helped form alliance with Catholic Center Party in Bavaria in 1891; supported German effort in World War I.

Vorwärts – daily central organ of Social Democratic Party in Germany; founded 1876.

Waldeck-Rousseau, René (1846–1904) – prime minister of France 1899–1902; headed "government of republican defense" that included Millerand.

Walecki, Henryk (1877–1937) – member of Polish SP from 1899; internationalist during World War I; took part in Zimmerwald Conference 1915; founding member of Polish CP 1919; assistant secretary to Comintern Balkan Secretariat 1928–35; editor in chief of *Communist International* 1935–37; arrested and executed during Stalin purges.

Wurm, Emmanuel (1857–1920) – joined German SPD 1880s; leading supporter with Kautsky of SPD "Marxist Center"; Reichstag deputy from 1890; supporter of centrist opposition within SPD after 1915; founding member of Independent Social Democratic Party (USPD); Prussian food minister 1918.

Zetkin, Clara (1857–1933) – joined German socialist movement 1878; cofounder of Second International 1889; a leader of its Marxist wing; editor of SPD's women's journal *Die Gleichheit* 1891–1917; campaigner for women's emancipation; secretary of International Socialist Women's Bureau from 1907; joined German CP 1919; headed Communist Women's Movement 1921–26; founder and editor of *Die Kommunistische Fraueninternationale* 1921–25; Executive Committee of Communist International member 1921–33; Reichstag member 1920–33.

Zietz, Luise (1865–1922) – joined Social Democratic Party 1892; a founding leader of German socialist women's movement; appointed to SPD Executive Committee 1908; secretary of SPD Executive Committee split 1912–16; split from SPD 1917 and joined Independent Social Democratic Party (USPD); opposed party decision to join Comintern in 1920.

List of Official Congress Proceedings

PARIS CONGRESS, 1889

In German: *Protokoll des Internationalen Arbeiter-Kongresses zu Paris. Abgehalten vom 14. bis 20. Juli 1889* (Nürnberg: Druck und Verlag von Worlein & Comp., 1890).

BRUSSELS CONGRESS, 1891

In French: *Congrès international ouvrier socialiste tenu à Bruxelles du 16 au 23 août 1891* (Brussels: Imprimerie Désiré Brismée, 1893).

In German: *Verhandlungen und Beschlüsse des Internationalen Arbeiterkongresses zu Brüssel* (Berlin: Verlag der Expédition des "Vorwärts," Berliner Volksblatt, 1893).

ZURICH CONGRESS, 1893

In German: *Protokoll des Internationalen Sozialistischen Arbeiterkongresses in der Tonhalle Zürich vom 6. bis 12. August 1893* (Zurich: Buchhandlung des Schweiz., Grütlivereins, 1894).

LONDON CONGRESS, 1896

In English: *International Socialist Workers and Trade Union Congress. London 1896* (London: The Twentieth Century Press Limited, n.d.).

In German: *Verhandlungen und Beschlüsse des Internationalen Sozialistischen Arbeiter- und Gewerkschafts-Kongresses zu London vom 27. July bis 1. August 1896* (Berlin: Verlag der Expedition der Buchhandlung Vorwärts, 1896).

PARIS CONGRESS, 1900

In French: *Cinquième congrès international tenu à Paris du 23 au 27 Septembre 1900* (Paris: Société Nouvelle de Librairie et d'Édition, 1901).

In German: *Internationaler Sozialisten-Kongress zu Paris, 23. bis 27. September 1900* (Berlin: Verlag der Expedition der Buchhandlung Vorwärts, 1900).

AMSTERDAM CONGRESS, 1904

In German: *Internationaler Sozialistenkongress zu Amsterdam, 14. bis 20. August 1904* (Berlin: Verlag der Expedition der Buchhandlung Vorwärts, 1904).

In French: *Sixième congrès socialiste international tenu à Amsterdam du 14 au 20 août 1904* (Brussels: Imprimerie Coopérative "Volksdrukkerij," 1904).

STUTTGART CONGRESS, 1907

In German: *Internationaler Sozialisten-Kongress, Stuttgart 1907, vom 18. bis 24. August 1907* (Berlin: Verlag Buchhandlung Vorwärts, 1907).

In French: *VIIe Congrès Socialiste International tenu à Stuttgart du 16 au 24 août 1907* (Brussels: Imprimerie-Lithographie Veuve Désiré Brismée, 1908).

COPENHAGEN CONGRESS, 1910

In French: *Huitième congrès socialiste international tenu à Copenhague du 28 août au 3 septembre 1910* (Brussels: Gand, Soc. Coop. "Volksdrukkerij").

In German: *Internationaler Sozialisten-Kongress zu Kopenhagen 28. August bis 3. September 1910* (Berlin: Verlag Buchhandlung Vorwärts, 1910).

BASEL CONGRESS, 1912

In German: *Ausserordentlicher Internationaler Sozialisten-Kongress zu Basel am 24. und 25. November 1912* (Berlin: Verlag Buchhandlung Vorwärts Paul Singer, G.m.b.H., 1912).

In French: *Compte rendu analytique du congrès socialiste international extraordinaire tenu à Bâle les 24 et 25 novembre 1912*, in *Bulletin Périodique du Bureau Socialiste International*, no. 10, n.d.

Notes

INTRODUCTION

1. From the president's address, given by Arthur Henderson, to the 1925 congress of the Labor and Socialist International. It can be found in John De Kay, *The Spirit of the International at Berne* (Bern: the author, 1919), 204.
2. V. I. Lenin, "The Position and Tasks of the Socialist International," reproduced as an appendix to this book.

MILLERANDISM

1. Eduard Bernstein, *Evolutionary Socialism* (New York: Schocken Books, 1961), 202.
2. Frederick Engels, letter to Filippo Turati, January 26, 1894, available at Marxists Internet Archive, https://www.marxists.org/archive/marx/works/1894/letters/94_01_26.htm.
3. Karl Kautsky, *The Road to Power* (1909), available at Marxists Internet Archive, https://www.marxists.org/archive/kautsky/1909/power/ch01.htm.
4. In 1894, French army captain Alfred Dreyfus, a Jew, was falsely convicted of treason for allegedly selling military secrets to Germany and was then sentenced by court-martial to life in prison. An anti-Semitic campaign was waged throughout France around the case, focusing on the supposed disloyalty of French Jews. A fight against the injustice to Dreyfus was waged by republican and anticlerical forces. A second court-martial was conducted in 1899, at which Dreyfus was sentenced to ten years' imprisonment, but he was soon pardoned and released. Nevertheless, the legal battle continued until 1906, when an appeals court set aside the judgment and fully exonerated Dreyfus.

   Within the socialist movement, the Dreyfus affair sparked important differences. Jean Jaurès championed the movement to defend Dreyfus, while Jules Guesde and his supporters took a sectarian position, viewing it simply as a fight between different factions of the bourgeoisie. "The proletarians for their part have no interest in this battle, which is not their own," Guesde stated. Quoted in Jean-Numa Ducange, *Jules Guesde: The Birth of Socialism in France* (London: Palgrave Macmillan, 2020), 89.
5. According to Wilhelm Liebknecht, "[a] Socialist who goes into a bourgeois government either goes over to the enemy or else puts himself in the power of

the enemy. In any case, the Socialist who becomes a member of a bourgeois government separates himself from us, the militant Socialists. He may claim to be a Socialist but he is no longer such. He may be convinced of his own sincerity, but in that case he has not comprehended the nature of the class struggle—does not understand that the class struggle is the basis of Socialism. . . . The unfortunate Socialist who casts in his lot with such a government, if he will not betray his class, only condemns himself to impotency." Wilhelm Liebknecht, "No Compromise, No Political Trading" (1899), in William A. Pelz (ed.), *Wilhelm Liebknecht and German Social Democracy: A Documentary History* (Chicago: Haymarket Books, 2016), 209.

6. In 1899, Kautsky wrote a lengthy polemic against Bernstein's views: "Bernstein und das Sozialdemokratische Programm: Eine Antikritik," available in German at Marxists Internet Archive, https://www.marxists.org/deutsch/archiv/kautsky/1899/bernstein/index.htm.
7. The Social Democratic Party congress of 1893 declared against the German party's participation in legislative elections under Prussia's reactionary three-class voting system. That position was reversed at the SPD's 1897 congress, and participation in elections to the Landtag (state assembly) was encouraged. "Participation in the next Prussian legislative elections is recommended everywhere the conditions render it possible for the party members to do so." That position was ratified at the 1898 congress. See Liebknecht, "No Compromise," in Pelz, *Wilhelm Liebknecht*, 180–82.
8. In the midst of the Franco-Prussian War of 1870–71, demands were raised in France for the formation of a republican government that could defend the country, replacing the imperial regime of Louis-Napoléon Bonaparte. These included calls for participation in such a government by left-wing republican forces and workers' representatives such as Louis-Auguste Blanqui and Charles Delescluze.
9. In the Prussian electoral system, voters were divided into three classes based on the amount of tax revenue paid. Since each of the three classes had the same electoral power, this in effect meant that a small minority of the wealthy elite had voting power equal to the vast majority of the population, consisting of the working class and other poor layers.
10. The Communist Manifesto states: "In Germany [the communists] fight with the bourgeoisie whenever it acts in a revolutionary way, against the absolute monarchy, the feudal squirearchy, and the petty bourgeoisie." See part IV on the "Position of the Communists in Relation to the Various Existing Opposition Parties."
11. Gaston Galliffet, minister of war in the Waldeck-Rousseau cabinet that included Millerand, was a French general who shared responsibility for the summary execution of thousands following the fall of the Paris Commune in 1871.
12. The Kishinev pogrom of April 1903 was one in a series of anti-Semitic attacks in tsarist Russia that received wide coverage in the world press, provoking an international outcry. Several thousand Jews were killed in these murderous onslaughts during the 1903–06 period, organized by monarchist elements with the support and complicity of the tsarist regime.
13. On April 23–26, 1905, a unity congress would be held in Paris between the two principal organizations of French socialism: the Socialist Party of France (PSDF) led by Jules Guesde and Édouard Vaillant, and the French Socialist Party (PSF) led by Jean Jaurès. The new united organization was formally named the Section française de l'Internationale ouvrière (French Section of the

Workers International, SFIO) but was known generally as the Socialist Party. The impetus for the unification came from the resolution on party unity adopted by the 1904 Amsterdam Congress, in Mike Taber (ed.), *Under the Socialist Banner: Resolutions of the Second International 1889–1912* (Chicago: Haymarket Books, 2021), 84–85.

14. The Left Bloc was formed in 1899, encompassing forces that had fought against the reactionary Dreyfus frame-up. Led by the Radical Party, it united left-bourgeois and some socialist forces in a parliamentary alliance. A Left Bloc government headed by Émile Combes held office from 1902 to 1905.

    Jaurès had greeted the 1902 formation of the Combes government, declaring: "We want to collaborate with the Left in a program of republican defense and social reforms; but at the same time, we intend to move toward those higher goals for which the proletariat has organized." Quoted in Harvey Goldberg, *The Life of Jean Jaurès* (Madison: University of Wisconsin Press, 1962), 294.
15. A congress of the French Workers Party (POF) held in Paris, December 3–8, 1899, adopted a resolution calling for socialists to accept only elective posts and to reject ministerial appointments, stating that "the class struggle does not allow a socialist to enter a bourgeois government." Quoted in Ducange, *Jules Guesde*, 95–96.
16. The Eighth Congress of the Italian Socialist Party was held in Bologna, April 8–11, 1904.
17. Giovanni Giolitti became Italy's prime minister in November 1903. Giolitti courted the Italian Socialist Party and sought unsuccessfully to have its leader, Filippo Turati, join his cabinet.
18. In the 1880s, German chancellor Otto von Bismarck began to put forward social welfare legislation as a way to counter the growing influence of the Social Democrats. These measures included insurance programs as well as limited regulation of child labor and workplace safety.
19. In the 1889 preface to his pamphlet *On the Political Position of Social Democracy*, Liebknecht wrote: "A general is inept if he is incapable of changing his plan of action in the course of a battle; many a brilliant victory has been won by a switch in tactics during the battle. . . . I have altered my tactics repeatedly, and it is quite possible that I will change them once more or perhaps even several times more. And I will certainly do so if the grounds or basis for it change." In Pelz, *Wilhelm Liebknecht*, 152.
20. A coalition was formed in the 1890s between Danish socialists and the Reform Venstre party. In 1901 this latter party was able to secure formation of a government.
21. Even though a national legislature existed in Sweden at the time, the country did not yet have a parliamentary system of government. Additionally, it was only in 1907 that suffrage was extended to all adult males; women did not obtain the vote until 1921.
22. This may be a reference to Ferdinand Lassalle's August 11, 1848, courtroom address, in which he stated: "When men hold their peace, the stones will cry out. When every human right is outraged, when even the ties of kinship are silent and a helpless being is abandoned by its natural protectors, then the first and the last relation of such a being has the right to rise in the person of another member of the human race."
23. On November 15, 1902, *Vorwärts*, the main daily newspaper of the SPD, printed a report that Friedrich Albert Krupp—head of the Krupp steel company—was

a homosexual and had had a number of affairs with men and boys. At that time, homosexual acts were illegal in Germany, punishable by years of imprisonment. Krupp died a week later, possibly by suicide. *Vorwärts* was publishing such scandal-mongering articles at the time as a way of showing the corruption of the bourgeoisie, even if some of these articles catered to backward prejudices.

24. An example of Bebel's point was the strike struggle by mine and metal workers in the Saône-et-Loire region of eastern France. In early 1901 Waldeck-Rousseau sent troops to the strike regions, allegedly to maintain order and protect private property. Jaurès was widely criticized within the labor movement for failing to criticize the government's actions.
25. While no member of Jaurès's Socialist Party of France actually joined Combes's Left Bloc government, this party became a pivotal force in it, especially during the 1903–04 period, when Jaurès was vice president of the Chamber of Deputies. The Socialist Party refused to break with this government, even after its naval armaments bills, its reliance on indirect taxes, its colonial agreements with Britain (the Entente Cordiale, signed in April 1904), and its use of the political police with a "secret fund."

    Secret funds were traditionally used by French governments to manipulate public opinion, to corrupt individuals, and to carry out other underhanded activities. Combes used such funds, among other purposes, to purge clerical supporters from the army. Jaurès voted for the fund, although Édouard Vaillant and other socialists were opposed, warning that it strengthened the political police.
26. A reference to the Amsterdam Congress resolution on party unity. For its text, see Taber, *Under the Socialist Banner*, 85–86.

COLONIALISM

1. Frederick Engels, speech on Poland, November 29, 1847, in *Marx Engels Collected Works*, vol. 6 (New York: International Publishers, 1976), 389.
2. The Second International's 1896 and 1900 resolutions on colonialism can be found in Mike Taber (ed.), *Under the Socialist Banner: Resolutions of the Second International 1889–1912* (Chicago: Haymarket Books, 2021), 52, 64, 72.
3. Quoted by Richard B. Day and Daniel Gaido (eds.), *Discovering Imperialism: Social Democracy to World War I* (Leiden: Brill, 2012), 11.
4. The 1904 resolution on India can be found in Taber, *Under the Socialist Banner*, 90.
5. Lenin was a member of the International Socialist Bureau—the Second International's executive body—for most of the time between 1905 and 1912, representing the Bolshevik wing of the Russian Social Democratic Labor Party.
6. V. I. Lenin, "Backward Europe and Advanced Asia," in *Collected Works*, vol. 19 (Moscow: Progress Publishers, 1980), 99–100.
7. The 1900 Paris Congress resolution on colonial policy had called for "socialist parties [to] apply themselves to the study of the colonial question wherever the economic conditions admit it." In Taber, *Under the Socialist Banner*, 72.
8. Joseph Chamberlain, secretary of state for the colonies, had come up with a number of schemes to expand the British Empire in Asia, Africa, and the West Indies.
9. During 1904–08, German troops were engaged in a genocidal war to defeat an uprising by the indigenous population of Germany's colony of South-West Africa, called "Hottentots" in colonialist lingo. The German Social Democrats opposed German colonialism during the war. During the election campaign of

January 1907—called the "Hottentot election"—the government and bourgeois parties waged a nationalist and chauvinist campaign against the SPD. The result was that the Social Democrats lost almost half of their Reichstag seats, which decreased from eighty-one to forty-three.

10. As a result of these remarks about "thieves' suppers," Quelch was ordered expelled from the German kingdom of Württemberg, where Stuttgart was located. For the remainder of the congress, Quelch's chair was kept empty and filled with flowers.
11. The passage from volume 3 of *Capital* reads: "From the standpoint of a higher economic form of society, private ownership of the globe by single individuals will appear quite as absurd as private ownership of one man by another. Even a whole society, a nation, or even all simultaneously existing societies taken together, are not the owners of the globe. They are only its possessors, its usufructuaries, and, like *boni patres familias*, they must hand it down to succeeding generations in an improved condition." Karl Marx, *Capital*, vol. 3, ch. 46, available at Marxists Internet Archive, https://www.marxists.org/archive/marx/works/1894-c3/ch46.htm.
12. Van Kol, a hydraulic engineer, had lived in Java for a number of years, purchasing a coffee plantation there in 1887. He gave part of the profits from the plantation to the Dutch labor movement.
13. The war in South Africa—known commonly as the Second Boer War—was fought from October 1899 to May 1902 between British troops and forces of the South African Republic (Transvaal) and Orange Free State. In this war, the British Empire sent almost half a million troops in an effort to strengthen its influence in southern Africa. Given Britain's military superiority, the Boer forces relied primarily on guerrilla tactics. British forces responded with extreme brutality, forcing civilian farmers and indigenous African residents into concentration camps, where many died.
14. Discussing the case of Russia, Marx and Engels considered it possible for societies with various precapitalist relations of production to bypass an extended stage of capitalist development, particularly in the event of successful proletarian revolutions in the advanced countries of Western Europe.
15. Formerly a Spanish colony, the Philippines was occupied by US forces in 1898 during the Spanish-American War. Upon Spain's surrender, a military occupation government was established. A brutal colonial war was waged by US troops between 1899 and 1902 against Filipino independence forces, causing hundreds of thousands of deaths.

IMMIGRATION

1. For more on Berger's racist views, see Mark Lisheron, "Victor Berger Virulent Bigot" at: https://www.badgerinstitute.org/Diggings/Spring-2019/Victor-Berger-Virulent-bigot.htm.
2. The 1893 and 1896 resolutions taking up the immigration question can be found in Mike Taber (ed.), *Under the Socialist Banner: Resolutions of the Second International 1889–1912* (Chicago: Haymarket Books, 2021), 42–43, 55, 64.
3. Georges Haupt (ed.), *Bureau Socialiste International: Comptes rendus des reúnions manifestes et circulares, 1900–1907* (Paris: Mouton & Co., 1969), 85–89.
4. The Bund was the General Union of Jewish Workers in Lithuania, Poland, and Russia.

5. In California, an anti-Japanese immigration law was passed by the state legislature in 1905, and in 1906 the children of Japanese immigrants were excluded from schools in the state. These measures were accompanied by riots and lynch attacks against Chinese and Japanese people.

WOMEN'S SUFFRAGE

1. The texts of these Second International resolutions can be found in Mike Taber (ed.), *Under the Socialist Banner: Resolutions of the Second International 1889–1912* (Chicago: Haymarket Books, 2021), 34, 44, 91.
2. In John Riddell (ed.), *To the Masses: Proceedings of the Third Congress of the Communist International, 1921* (Chicago: Haymarket Books, 2016), 780.
3. The Manheim Congress of the German Social Democratic Party took place September 23–29, 1906.
4. In March 1907, parliamentary elections were held for the first time in Finland—then under the control of the tsarist empire in Russia—in which women voted. The Finnish Social Democratic Party received the largest number of votes in these elections.
5. Proposals to add a point on women's suffrage to the congress agenda had been made by the socialist women's movments in Germany and in Austria.

MILITARISM AND WAR

1. The Fashoda Incident of September 18, 1898—the climax of a series of territorial disputes between the British and French colonial empires in Africa—involved a military standoff between British and French troops in Fashoda in Egyptian Sudan. Following the incident, the two powers eventually came to an agreement on the boundaries of their respective spheres of influence.

   The Morocco crisis of 1905–06 was rooted in the April 1904 formation of the Entente Cordiale by France and Britain to advance their respective interests in North Africa. France subsequently signed a secret treaty with Spain to partition Morocco. The German rulers, however, had their own designs and declared for Moroccan independence, leading to the first Moroccan crisis and sparking the threat of war between Germany and France. The crisis was resolved at a conference in Algeciras, which acknowledged Germany's economic interests while entrusting France and Spain with policing Morocco.

   The first Balkan War, from October to December 1912, was waged by Serbia, Bulgaria, Greece, and Montenegro against the Ottoman Empire. Under the terms of a May 1913 peace treaty, the Ottoman Empire lost almost all of its remaining European territory. A second Balkan War was waged from June to August 1913, with Serbia and Greece defeating Bulgaria over division of the territory conquered from the Ottoman Empire in Macedonia.
2. First International resolutions are quoted from G. M. Stekoff, *History of the First International* (New York: Russell & Russell, 1928), 86, 106, 121–22.
3. Karl Marx, "First Address of the General Council of the International Working Men's Association on the Franco-Prussian War," in *Marx Engels Collected Works*, vol. 22 (Moscow: Progress Publishers, 1986), 6.
4. Karl Marx, "The Civil War in France," in *Marx Engels Collected Works*, vol. 22, 331.

5. The Second International's militarism resolutions of 1896 and 1900 can be found in Mike Taber (ed.), *Under the Socialist Banner: Resolutions of the Second International 1889–1912* (Chicago: Haymarket Books, 2021), 55–56, 71.
6. For a version of the 1907 militarism resolution that highlights the amendments put forward by Luxemburg, Lenin, and Martov, see Taber, *Under the Socialist Banner*, 157–59.
7. Quoted in John Riddell (ed.), *Lenin's Struggle for a Revolutionary International* (New York: Pathfinder Press, 1984), 56.
8. Quotes by Noske and Kautsky are taken from Richard B. Day and Daniel Gaido (eds.), *Discovering Imperialism: Social Democracy to World War I* (Leiden: Brill, 2012), 34–35.
9. Rosa Luxemburg, "Peace Utopias," in *Rosa Luxemburg Speaks* (New York: Pathfinder Press, 1970), 254.
10. The Second International's Interparliamentary Committee was composed of socialist deputies in the parliaments of each country. It generally held its conferences alongside meetings of the International Socialist Bureau.
11. Bebel is referring to Rosa Luxemburg's opposition to the demand for national self-determination and independence in Poland, most of which was ruled by tsarist Russia.
12. Alsace-Lorraine was ceded by France to Germany in 1871 following the Franco-Prussian War. It was returned to France in 1919 but held by Nazi Germany from 1940 to 1945.
13. The Ems Dispatch was a falsified version of a meeting between King William of Prussia and the French ambassador, who met in 1870 at Ems, Prussia, to discuss the dispute between their two countries over influence in Spain. A dispatch summarizing the meeting was sent to German leader Otto von Bismarck, who edited it so as to offend French Emperor Napoleon III. Bismarck published this truncated version—a dispatch that provided the immediate pretext for the Franco-Prussian War of 1870–71.
14. Karl Liebknecht's book *Militarism and Anti-Militarism* was published in February 1907. On April 17, the Prussian war minister instituted legal proceedings against Liebknecht, who was charged with high treason, accused of having advocated the "abolition of the standing army by means of the military strike, if needs be conjointly with the incitement of troops to take part in the revolution" and "organically disintegrating and demoralizing the militarist spirit." Liebknecht was convicted in October 1907 and subsequently imprisoned for eighteen months.
15. During the Morocco crisis, socialists in Germany and France organized meetings and demonstrations to protest the threat of war. A public meeting organized by the SPD in Berlin on July 9, 1905, for example, invited Jean Jaurès to speak. However, Germany's chancellor prohibited the latter's participation in the meeting.
16. The congress of French Socialists at Nancy held August 11–14, 1907, the week before the Stuttgart Congress, witnessed a debate on militarism. Hervé supported a resolution backed by Jaurès, with its key provision adopted by a vote of 169 to 125, in opposition to a resolution supported by Guesde.
17. Hervé is referring here to Bebel's remarks at the 1904 Amsterdam Congress comparing and contrasting bourgeois republics with monarchies. See chapter 1.
18. Bebel and Wilhelm Liebknecht, the two Social Democratic members of the Reichstag, had refused to vote for war appropriations and had opposed

Germany's annexation of Alsace and Lorraine. They were tried for high treason in 1872, owing, among other things, to their expressed support for the Paris Commune, and were sentenced to two-year prison terms.

19. Rosa Luxemburg had already been jailed a number of times. In July 1904, she had been sentenced to three months' imprisonment in Germany for "insulting the emperor." She had also been jailed in Russian Poland during the 1905–06 revolution. Luxemburg was imprisoned again during June and July of 1907 for making allegedly seditious remarks at the SPD's 1905 congress at Jena.
20. The French expression "working for the king of Prussia" refers to labor from which the advantages are reaped by others. The term originated out of the peace of 1748, which brought France no gains, while France's ally Prussia annexed the rich province of Silesia.
21. Prior to the 1905 unification that created a united socialist party in France, Jaurès and Vaillant had been leaders of different organizations within the French socialist movement.
22. During the nineteenth century, Italy waged a series of independence wars against the Habsburg Empire of Austria. Unification of Italy was completed in 1871.
    German unification was also completed in 1871 following the Franco-Prussian War. The expression "blood and iron" is a reference to a speech given in 1862 by Prussian minister president Otto von Bismarck, who was to lead Germany's unification under Prussian domination.
23. An indoor peace rally was held in Paris on October 29, 1900, sponsored by the French trade unions. Some two to three thousand people packed the hall, shouting, "Down with war!" Leaders of the British unions spoke and delivered a message of support passed by the British Trades Union Congress the previous month. The Paris meeting passed a resolution supporting "the fraternal union of the workers of the two countries" and demanding that disputes between France and Britain "should be settled by arbitration."
24. The Anti-Socialist Laws were passed in 1878 by the German government of Chancellor Otto von Bismarck. While not banning the Social Democratic Party outright, these laws outlawed the propagation of the SPD's views through the press and public meetings, and banned its local organizations and all Social Democratic–led trade unions, allowing only parliamentary activity. Through its underground activities and by taking advantage of legal openings that remained, however, the SPD was able to grow greatly in membership and influence. In 1890, under pressure from the rising working-class movement, the laws were repealed.
25. The quote is from Wilhelm Liebknecht's remarks at the 1893 Second International congress in Zurich. *Protokoll des Internationalen Sozialistischen Arbeiterkongresses in der Tonhalle Zürich vom 6. bis 12. August 1893* (Zurich: Buchhandlung des Schweiz., Grutlivereins, 1894), 25.
26. The war between Russia and Japan, which grew out of a rivalry for dominance in Korea and Manchuria, lasted from February 1904 to September 1905, ending in a victory for Japan.
27. The revanchist movement in France was strong in the 1880s and 1890s, with widespread anti-German sentiment over the seizure of Alsace and Lorraine following the Franco-Prussian War of 1870–71. At the time, Guesde stood up to the French nationalist right wing, proudly asserting his ties with the German workers' movement.

28. Baroness Bertha von Suttner was an Austrian-Czech pacifist awarded the Nobel Peace Prize in 1905.
29. The Amsterdam Congress resolution on the general strike can be found in Taber, *Under the Socialist Banner*, 85–86.
30. The SPD's Jena Congress of September 17–23, 1905, influenced by the revolutionary events in Russia, was the scene of a turn by the SPD toward the left in its adopted resolutions. The most important such resolution was on the question of the mass strike, put forward by Bebel. For the first time at a congress of the SPD, a resolution spoke of the mass strike as a weapon that could be used by the working class. The adoption of this resolution was a rebuff to the revisionist wing of the party, of which Vollmar was a leader.
31. During the spring and summer of 1907, Belfast was rocked by a militant strike carried out by dockworkers, which was spreading to other sections of the working class. Contrary to Russell Smart's claim, on August 12, British troops did in fact fire on a crowd of three to five hundred in Belfast's Catholic district, killing two and wounding twelve.
32. The final sentence of the resolution on war adopted by the 1907 French SP congress in Nancy urged antiwar action "by all means—from parliamentary intervention, public agitation, and popular demonstrations, up to a workers' general strike and insurrection."
33. On May 21–22, 1905, a summit meeting was held in Trieste (then in Austria-Hungary) between Italian and Austrian socialist leaders, headed by Leonida Bissolati and Victor Adler, to discuss a coordinated response in case war broke out between the two countries.
34. In 1905, following the Norwegian declaration of independence from Sweden, mass working-class mobilizations in Sweden helped prevent a war by that country's ruling class against Norway.
35. The social crisis resulting from the Russo-Japanese War of 1904–05 was a factor leading to the outbreak of the revolution of 1905 throughout the tsarist empire.
36. Marx drafted three addresses on the Franco-Prussian War on behalf of the General Council of the International Workingmen's Association (the First International). The third of these, published as *The Civil War in France*, gives Marx's fullest account of the development and consequences of the war. These addresses can all be found in volume 22 of *Marx Engels Collected Works*.
37. Right-wing British socialist Henry Hyndman, an advocate for "a powerful navy for Great Britain," was calling for a £100 million naval loan.
38. Radek is presumably referring to three front-page articles in the August 1–3 issues of *Leipzeiger Volkzeitung*. The first article was "Flottenabkommen" (Fleet agreement); the second and third were titled "Das englisch-deutsche Kapital und das Flottenabkommen" (English-German capital and the fleet agreement). The article from *Vorwärts* to which Radek was replying was probably "Der englische Verständigungsversuch" (The English attempt at an agreement an unsigned front-page article about disarmament published in *Vorwärts*, August 5, 1910.)
39. During the American Civil War of 1861–65, Britain gave underhanded support to the Confederacy. One example of the assistance given by Confederate supporters in Britain was helping to provide warships that could be used in breaking the Union blockade of Confederate states. One such ship, the CSS *Alabama*, was especially notorious for its campaign of piracy, capturing and burning dozens

of US vessels. After the war an international tribunal compelled Britain to pay $15.5 million in damages to US shipping interests.

40. Former US president Theodore Roosevelt traveled to Egypt in March 1910 as part of a hunting safari to Africa. While there, he made a well-publicized address attacking Egyptian nationalism.
41. The Hague conferences of 1899 and 1907, with over two dozen governments participating, produced a series of international treaties on naval and land armaments and weaponry, with provisions for creating a Permanent Court of Arbitration.

APPENDIX: LENIN ON TRENDS

1. "The International Socialist Congress in Stuttgart" is taken from V. I. Lenin, *Collected Works*, vol. 13 (Moscow: Progress Publishers, 1972), 75–81; the second version, under the same title, is also in vol. 13, 82–93. "The Position and Tasks of the Socialist International" can be found in vol. 21 (Moscow: Progress Publishers, 1977), 35–41.
2. Karl Marx, *Capital*, vol. 1, chapter 24, available at Marxists Internet Archive.
3. The bracketed paragraphs here are taken from Lenin's second article on the Stuttgart Congress, which can be found in Lenin, *Collected Works*, vol. 13, 82–93.
4. Deleted here is a long section on the trade union discussion at Stuttgart, which had particular relevance for Lenin's readers at the time, as they involved disagreements between Bolsheviks and Mensheviks then preoccupying the Russian socialist movement.
5. Lenin here goes on to examine in detail the situation of the socialist movement in each of the major countries.

Index

Page numbers in italics signify remarks by individuals to Second International congresses.

About Haymarket Books

Haymarket Books is a radical, independent, nonprofit book publisher based in Chicago.

Our mission is to publish books that contribute to struggles for social and economic justice. We strive to make our books a vibrant and organic part of social movements and the education and development of a critical, engaged, international left.

We take inspiration and courage from our namesakes, the Haymarket martyrs, who gave their lives fighting for a better world. Their 1886 struggle for the eight-hour day—which gave us May Day, the international workers' holiday—reminds workers around the world that ordinary people can organize and struggle for their own liberation. These struggles continue today across the globe—struggles against oppression, exploitation, poverty, and war.

Since our founding in 2001, Haymarket Books has published more than five hundred titles. Radically independent, we seek to drive a wedge into the risk-averse world of corporate book publishing. Our authors include Noam Chomsky, Arundhati Roy, Rebecca Solnit, Angela Y. Davis, Howard Zinn, Amy Goodman, Wallace Shawn, Mike Davis, Winona LaDuke, Ilan Pappé, Richard Wolff, Dave Zirin, Keeanga-Yamahtta Taylor, Nick Turse, Dahr Jamail, David Barsamian, Elizabeth Laird, Amira Hass, Mark Steel, Avi Lewis, Naomi Klein, and Neil Davidson. We are also the trade publishers of the acclaimed Historical Materialism Book Series and of Dispatch Books.

CPSIA information can be obtained
at www.ICGtesting.com
Printed in the USA
JSHW021149090623
42977JS00004B/4

9 781642 599817